A MOTHER'S WISDOM

A Collection of Wise Words from Mothers

Edited by: CATHRYN J. LOMBARDO

Goodnight Publishing
http://www.GoodnightPublishing.com

A Mother's Wisdom is a collection of wise words from mothers across the United States.

Published in the United States of America through:
Goodnight Publishing
www.GoodnightPublishing.com

info@GoodnightPublishing.com

© 2011 by Cathryn J. Lombardo
Cover Design by Ruth Perkins
Author Photo by SC Lawrence Photography

All rights reserved. No part of this book may be used or reproduced in any form or by any means without the prior written consent of the Publisher, except for brief quotations used in critical articles or reviews. Please do not participate in or encourage piracy of copyrighted materials (including e-books) in violation of author's rights. Purchase only authorized editions.

Goodnight Publishing and its Logo are Registered Trademarks.

ISBN-13: 9781456528850
EAN-10: 1456528858

DEDICATED to the memory of my mother, Mary, and my mother-in-law, Giovanna, who both passed away in December, 2009, and who both gave me tremendous advice and bushels of love.

Also dedicated to mothers everywhere – your wisdom is a precious commodity which will always remain alive, needed, and cherished.

EDITOR'S NOTE

This book could never have been produced if it weren't for the tremendous contributions of the twenty-seven mothers who so graciously and diligently wrote their unique messages for all to share. I am in their debt.

Since this is a book composed of loving letters, poems and a collection of thoughts, I have kept each author's voice as true to her as possible. Any and all mistakes found are mine.

It is with hope and faith that whoever reads this book does so in the heartfelt manner in which it was both written and compiled.

Cathryn J. Lombardo, *Editor*

Table of Contents

Title/Author	Page
Advice to My Child, Laurie Schnebly-Campbell	1
A Mother's Wisdom – Diane, Diane Mockbee	5
Nurturing Others & Yourself, Shirley Blaul	9
The Magical World of Motherhood, Shannon Zweig	15
A Mother's Wisdom – Karen, Karen Applegate	23
For My Sons, Cathryn J. Lombardo	25
A Mother's Wisdom – Peggy, Peggy Lee Miller	33
A Mother's Wisdom – Julie, Julie Blatz	39
Motherhood is Survival of the Craziest, Stacey Goitia	43
From the Journal of Gypsy Le Fai, Gypsy Le Fai	49
A Mother's Wisdom – Jackie, Jackie Karras	53
For Ian, Donna Del Grosso	57
My Family's Particular Wisdom, Jeanne Cook	63
My Gift to My Grandchildren, Lynda Demos	69
A Mother's Advice, Lee Schnebly	77
A Mother's Wisdom – Valeria, Dr. Valeria Breiten	81
Children Are Hilarious, Kris Tualla	85
My Dearest Babies, Abby Prentice	91
Stubbornness as a Virtue, Nancy Chaney	95
A Mom's Haiku to My Two Plus Five Words of Wisdom, Connie Flynn	101
Life Isn't Fair...Suck It Up!, Kayce Lassiter	107
A Mother's Wisdom – Iris, Iris Sperry	113

Title/Author	Page
A Most Wise Woman – My Mother, Jaylene Nuttall	**117**
To My Children and Grandchildren, Nancy Andrews	**121**
A Mother's Wisdom – Bette, Elizabeth McNicholas	**127**
For My Children – An Alphabet of Lessons I've Learned From Life, Shelley Mosley	**131**
Here's to the Journey!! – On BEING Your Mom, Mary J. Neuman	**139**

Acknowledgements	**145**
Contributing Author Websites	**146**
References	**148**

A Mother's Wisdom

Advice to My Child

While all these events are still a ways off in your life, here's what I want you to know about each milestone:

FIRST YEAR OF MARRIAGE

There'll be times when the relationship soars, and times when it limps. Both are normal; both are okay. As a newlywed I used to think there was something wrong if your dad and I weren't shimmering with joy in each other's company every hour of the day, and gradually came to realize that a marriage goes through the same kind of up-and-down waves as the weather patterns. So don't worry when you're in a down-wave; things WILL bounce up again in another few weeks.

And my other piece of advice is for when you've been married one month – make THAT the time you get your saved-from the-wedding cake out of the freezer and eat it, because after a year in the freezer it won't be worth eating!

BECOMING A PARENT

You'll discover it's tempting to think that this new baby is an extension of YOU. But that's not the case. This new baby is his or her own person, and deserves the same kind of respect-for-individuality you'd give any other loved one who isn't you.

So if your kid prefers a different kind of activity or friends or style than you do, it's okay. You don't have to indulge every preference expressed, but do respect the fact that this kid is not you!

I remember telling people that when you grew up, I couldn't take the credit if you turned out to be a Nobel laureate any more than I could take the blame if you turned out to be a bum. Our job as parents was to give you the best life-tools we could, but making use of them is your job... and you've done a FABULOUS job of it. Which, again, is more because of your own personality – the uniquely cool person you are – than because of our terrific parenting.

Respect each of your kids as an individual, and LOVE each one as an individual, and whatever you do as a parent from there on out will be fine.

EMPTY-NESTING

Still moving on to when your first and/or last kid leaves home, a quick piece of advice to keep the transition from being a tough thing to get through: go on vacation. We discovered that by accident the week after you left for college, having coincidentally planned a business trip for me with your dad coming along for fun. Being together as a Couple reconnected us with the time before we became a Family-With-Children, reminding us why we loved each other in the first place, and made it a lot easier to get through the transition from Family back to Couple.

Same thing if you're on your own when your kid leaves home...do something that reminds you there's still a life of your own waiting for you to enjoy it. You'll still miss your away-from-home child, sure, but it's a lot less painful when you have something to snap you into a whole new frame of mind shortly after that last wave good-bye.

LOSS OF LOVED ONES

All of us, your parents and grandparents alike, know how VERY much you've meant to us (and vice versa). So if you don't get a chance to say the perfect thing at the last minute, know that we won't feel cheated -- we already knew it!

You've been the best thing in my life, and I'm so glad you're the person you are. Whether you hear it from me in person or

Cathryn J. Lombardo

just remember hearing it anytime you think about "what would Mom say," know that loving you has been my greatest joy. And I love thinking that someday you'll share that joy yourself...because I can't think of any experience more wonderful than being happy with who your child is.

Thanks, pie.
Love, Mom

Laurie - one son

A Mother's Wisdom – Diane

I waited five years of marriage to have a child and to begin our family. My firstborn was a precious little girl, Lisa, who brought so much joy into my life. I remember rocking her at night and thinking what a miracle she was. My heart abounded with so much love and I knew right then that she was someone very special. She grew into a very active and happy little girl, full of giggles and delight over everything she encountered. She welcomed her baby brother, Sean, in much the same way she welcomed any new experience – with joy and love.

I thought I could never love anyone as much as I loved Lisa, but when Sean came along, I knew I had been wrong. I loved him just as much as I did Lisa, and my heart swelled again as I looked down into his sweet and innocent face. I love each child equally. Each of them is special to me in their own way; I never loved one more than the other. (Though, over the years that has been debated by my kids!)

Cathryn J. Lombardo

As they grew, I made some mistakes as a mother and I was not perfect, yet I seemed to always remain perfect in their eyes. Throughout grade school, junior high, high school and college, we continued to grow together. Of course, there were times when, according to them, I didn't know anything; but, as they grew into adulthood, I became so much smarter! Today, if they want advice, I will give it. I do not force my ideas on them or tell them they are "wrong" in what they are doing. Instead, I am there to listen, to provide support and to offer assistance when it is needed or asked for. My own mother set that example for me. She was always there for me, listening, loving and showing me what family is all about. She created wonderful traditions which I have instilled in my own kids. My mother has always been the basis of much of my own mothering techniques. I owe her so much and still wish we could talk every day, BUT...my memories prevail!

I always believed that if my children were raised with love in a Christian home, they would become the person God intended them to be. Of course, there were times that I was unsure of the path they were on, but each child made choices that were right for them and one each was very happy with. I have always had so much pride in all of their endeavors no matter what they were. When their college years arrived, Lisa chose to leave home and Sean chose to stay. These were exciting times for them as they became adults and discovered their future paths. My heart swelled with love and pride when they received their diplomas. By this time, Lisa and Sean's love for me seemed to only grow as they began their own individual lives as mature adults. It also seemed their appreciation for *me* as a mother was more abundant.

As I watch them raise their own children, I'm delighted to see how Lisa and Sean have become great parents in their own right. Lisa is the mother of four beautiful children and Sean the father of one handsome little boy. Of course they make mistakes, but the love they have for their children is like the love I have always had for them – it is unconditional. They are so proud to share the lives of their children with me as a grandmother and this couldn't make me happier! Now as they are raising their children, they too will make mistakes, but their children's love for them will never change.

As a mother and grandmother, the love I have for my children and grandchildren continues on and I know that love will continue for generations to come.

Diane – one daughter and one son; five grandchildren.

Cathryn J. Lombardo

Nurturing Others and Yourself

To *nurture* (from my crossword-puzzlers dictionary) means: "to feed and care for during growth."[1] My hope is that your lives will be ones of nurturing both yourselves and all of your relationships.

In your marriage and family life, it is special if you and your loved ones share *common* interests so that you can enjoy the same activities. However, your children will undoubtedly prove that each one is unique and in need of their own individual encouragement as you allow them to develop their desires and strengths. But I carry my wish even further to include you, the adult. Besides being a nurturing spouse and parent, I hope that you will develop your own "personhood" to include *your* own individual interests, hobbies and pastimes. Your father/grandfather and I were pleased that we "celebrated our differences." Not only can these personal differences enrich your marriage and family, but if you should become single as I now am, you may have an easier time carrying on your life alone. I'm finding that as long as health and resources permit, it is never too late to take a class, travel, learn a new craft or be a volunteer for a cause that speaks to your heart.

Another feature of nurturing is how we treat our loved ones in *public*. I am saddened when I hear people berating (putting down, even in jest) their spouse or child in front of others. This is not only damaging to the "victim," but it makes the audience uncomfortable and often unable to intervene. Wouldn't it be better if our criticisms could always be constructive, loving, and given in private?

Gratitude serves as another way of showing how much we appreciate others for who they are and for what they do. Also, it turns our own thoughts towards the blessings and positive aspects of our lives and away from those negative thoughts.

The act of *forgiveness* is also a path of nurturing – not that the "fault" needs to be condoned or even forgotten, but forgiveness brings freedom from bitterness and can often restore the damaged relationship.

Friendships give us many opportunities to be recipients and givers of nurturing. As an only child (I prefer to think of myself as a "limited edition"), friends have always played a very important part of my life. And because I enjoy writing, I have stayed in touch with many friends over the years.

Of course, I'm aware that emails, texting, and Facebook are used by your generations to keep in touch. These obviously have their merits, but I'd like to put in a good word for telephone calls and written letters because of their more personal, private and one-on-one nature.

I'm sure you won't be surprised to learn that Christmas card exchanging is my favorite holiday activity. In fact, I have taken this a step further by sending these postcards:

> *Dear _____*
> *Several years ago I began remembering friends (and their families) on their own special* **Day of Gratitude, Thought, and Prayer.** *These dates have been randomly chosen from the holiday card I received and saved. I am thankful you are part of my life!*
>
> *You will be in my thoughts and prayers on (*I add the date*)*

The blessings I receive are that I get to recall how these friends have impacted my life and the memories we share, as well as re-reading their holiday newsletter and praying for them. And this often leads to another exchange of communication.

Cathryn J. Lombardo

There are many different levels of friendships and each one can add to our lives. From the movie "Six Degrees of Separation,"[2] comes this thought: "Every person is a new door to a different world." In addition to those few close friends currently in your lives, others may include the casual acquaintances you know through your children or a club you belong to, co-workers, neighbors; those who share common interests like a knitting or book group; and even friends from your past.

A quote by Elizabeth Foley[3] I found on "Friendship Quotes" touched me: "The most beautiful discovery that true friends can make is that they can grow separately without growing apart." This has proven true of a group of my sixteen college friends who met fifty-eight years ago, and who now live in all parts of our country. In 1993, we started having reunions every two to three years. I think we are still close because we not only validate each other's growth over the years – we rejoice in it.

At this time in my life I am living alone and separated by many miles from you, my family. Without friends and activities, I could become a lonely old lady who no longer nurtures others or herself. But, thankfully, my life is busy and filled with a variety of acquaintances, close neighbors, church members and prayer partners, enjoyable companions and one very close friend. Although we are not sisters by birth, I feel we are sisters by heart.

Last, but by no means least, the epitome of nurturing yourself and others is faith in God. I personally have known His love, comfort, strength and guidance over the years and would wish for you, your own walk with Him.

Shirley – one daughter; two granddaughters; one great-grandson

Cathryn J. Lombardo

A Mother's Wisdom

The Magical World of Motherhood

On a typically rainy day in Portland, Oregon my husband was engrossed by the televised battle between the Green Bay Packers and the Minnesota Vikings. I was locked in a closet doubling as a bathroom, entranced by the creeping neon blue dye flowing in a straight line on a white plastic stick. The cheers from the living room fade into the background as a mixture of shock and excitement run through me. Our lives were about to change. We repeated the blue line incident two years later and now after eight more years have passed, the depth of those changes still amaze me. Motherhood is a balancing act of those things you lose with those you gain.

There are two stages to my life: B.C.: Before Children and A.C.: After Children. There's a reason historians separated our timeline with the birth of Jesus, people. Children bring you great joy, but the only way you can feel the depth of such love and bliss is to fully appreciate the sacrifices the unique experience entails.

Let's start with the first item up on your sacrificial alter, your clothes. I lost the ability to wear white. I'm not talking about just after Labor Day; I'm talking about in any point and time. It's not because I'm a slob, but it became an instant blank canvas for my two demons...sorry, I mean boys. Those endearing "Mommy, hug please?" complete with dewy filled big eyes were just a cover. I'd wrap my arms around them only to find some mysterious substance spreading across the once pristine, clean white cloth. There was a time B.C., where my wardrobe included colorful, feminine apparel. Today, I fend off threats from a single friend to buy me a fluorescent pink shirt to offset the drab blue, green, and gray colors dominating my closet. B.C., it was facing the challenge of creating a flattering outfit each morning. A.C., it's more of which of my dark shirts will hide the most dirt the longest. The upside to this particular sacrifice is twofold. First, I'm always comfortable. No pinched toes or strained arches, besides tennis shoes offer much more traction in chasing after my boys. No outfit is tight since the ability to twist into many positions, which would make a yoga master envious, is an everyday occurrence. More importantly, now when I dress up, my husband notices.

The second item up for forfeiture was my music. I love music, the louder the better. B.C., I lived to drive with my windows down, wind fingering my hair. The stereo would be pounding out driving beats with me trying my karaoke best to accompany the lyrics as I discovered little out-of-the-way places and new scenery. The freedom to sing at the top of my lungs about the devious man who broke my heart or turned me on, has become few and very far between. Now, I'm an agent of the FCC. Early on, I was reduced to listening to aging Australian men singing about dinosaurs and spaghetti. Where's the fun in that? Dorothy the Dinosaur just doesn't give the same expressive satisfaction as, say, Three Days Grace or Seether. Granted, my boys no longer find anything amusing or entertaining with dancing dinosaurs and men in color coordinated outfits, but censorship is alive and well in my mini-van. I've also begun channeling my mother as I find myself wondering, at which point did a song require the descriptive use of cuss words? I could swear it wasn't this bad B.C., but maybe I couldn't hear those words over the wind in my ears!

With the arrival of my boys, the ability to find some quiet "alone" time seems to have gone the way of the do-do bird. B.C., I could escape to the coffee shop, sit, write and people-watch hours on end. Now, I'm lucky to scrape a few hours away each week just to breathe in the luscious scents of Starbucks. Somehow, between the demands of my tele-commuting job, holding a phone conference (all hail the mute button), and solving World War III involving who really won the last Mario Brothers' challenge on the *Wii*, my creative spark is mashed into a small pile of mush under a muddy tennis shoe which has been left in the middle of the hallway.

You've seen those commercials where the mother, dressed to the nines in her spotless white Capri pants and pretty, feminine shirt, with not one strand of beautiful hair out of place, sits in her immaculately clean house, enjoying a pristine moment of perfect, calming solitude, sipping a hot cup of cappuccino, while her obviously enchanted children play on the photographic green lawn. I swear I'm not a violent person but the urge to maim has never been as commanding as it is when that commercial comes on. You and I both know it's some male behind the idea, because any rational female understands it is so far from reality, it's laughable. Reality is a mom dressed in jeans and one of her husband's dark t-shirts, with no make-up hiding the sleepless night before, while her house looks as if the two small tornados outside have just blown through it. And that perfect cup of cappuccino? It's instant coffee and it's cold. The shrieks outside making the windows rattle in the kitchen? Proof that sugar is not a good additive to any food group.

Yet for all the sacrifices we make when we welcome our little bundle of joys into this world, we all have to agree, it's worth every stained shirt, every grey hair, every minute you spend picking up behind them, because they are our magic. I never spent much time thinking about my parenting techniques B.C. Now that my boys are ten and nine, I've uncovered the origins of my skills as a parent, my mom. Or, in my case: moms.

My biological mom passed away when I was six, but she left some strong impressions behind. She showed me patience, endurance, and love as she struggled to raise a child on her own after a difficult divorce. Her biggest gift to me was opening my eyes to a world beyond our own with her magical explanations of everyday happenings:

> *"Mommy, where do freckles come from?"*
> *"Well, love, at night when you're asleep, little brownie fairies come and leave you kisses. Those little kisses turn into freckles."*
> *"And the little red ones?"*
> *"Those are special rose kisses. Not many little girls get those. You must be as special to them as you are to me."*

When I was twelve, my second mom stepped into my life and finished what my biological mother had started. Through her faith, love and belief in me, she helped to create the foundation of the woman I'd become. She never let my youthful arrogance deter her. My useless vows of how I would never ask my children such questions like, "If all your friends were jumping off a cliff, would you?" are now ashes in the wind, especially since I found her voice emerging from my mouth with that same question a few months ago with my oldest. What's even more humbling, he responded, "Well, no, Mom, that would be stupid." In the end, both of these strong women left their marks.

The first night I held my oldest in my arms, I cried. There were tears of joy I shared with my mom as she stood beside me, but a small part was a little six-year-old wishing her other mom was still around. Since then I've tried to share the magic of the kissing fairies, the strength of acceptance and endurance as you face life's challenges, and the grace and love their grandmother has blessed me with every day for the last twenty-eight years.

For all the changes my boys' arrivals have created, I keep close to my heart the memories of watching them held spellbound by the words of Star Wars as their dad read to them each night; or those times I pushed aside my keyboard to join in the coloring-fest where the sky was yellow and the trees red. Even today, I thrill to the sound of their laughter when they discover some newfound ability they didn't think they'd conquer.

When memories of my childhood peek out, I find comfort in recognizing both of my moms in their quick wit and vivid imaginations. Their innate strength to be uniquely themselves brings sunlight to my soul. As long as I still get to hold my oldest son's hand and dance to our music blasting through my messy house, or spend a few precious moments with my youngest building the next Lego masterpiece, I'll gladly give up wearing white and sipping coffee in perfect silence. Maybe those fairies were on to something, because somehow two very magnificent boys chose me for a mom, and I'll make whatever sacrifices required to keep them as mine.

Shannon – two sons

Cathryn J. Lombardo

A Mother's Wisdom - Karen

First of all, I must say that I am truly blessed to still have my mother around with me at the delicate age of ninety-five years old. I am able to see and experience both worlds as a mother of a wonderful daughter, and as a daughter of a wonderful mother.

So my wisdom/knowledge which I wish to share is: as a mother speaks to you from her heart, she is simply trying to guide you in the right direction using her many, many years of experience to help you travel through your life with less mistakes and heartaches.

It is so easy to be on the receiving end of all this wisdom and feel that your mother is trying to run or control your life. What wisdom she shares with you comes from deep down in her heart because a mother's love is always there.

Karen – one daughter and one son; grandchildren

Cathryn J. Lombardo

A Mother's Wisdom

For My Sons

I never dreamed I would become a mother because I never thought I would be married. I always saw myself joining the diplomatic corps where I would be permanently stationed in Vienna, Austria; and if I should become an aunt, would become that "grand dame" who taught her nieces and nephews the nuances of European society. Obviously *that* didn't happen. Instead, I did marry and was blessed with three incredible sons, each one unique and independent. Just know that you, my dear sons, are precious jewels to me. You have grown to be fine men and great sources of inspiration in my life. Even though your life's journey has already begun, here is some wisdom I would like to share to help you along the way.

Communication: In any relationship, the better able you are to communicate your thoughts and desires without resorting to intimidation, anger, fear-mongering, etc. the better your life will be. There are always TWO sides to an issue. Communication is about LISTENING, which means stopping *your* litany long enough to understand the other's point of view. No one wants to be "talked over" by another. Each person's (yours included) ideas, feelings, and actions are valid and need to be treated as such.

Compromise: To me, it is the antithesis of the "All about Me" syndrome. We get stuck in ourselves, who we are, what we want/need and so doing, choose not to notice what we are doing to others around us. Nothing is worse than someone who insists on imposing their will upon another. In any relationship, BOTH sides need consideration. Respecting each other's needs and acting accordingly will serve you well.

Love: What is love really? Is it a feeling, an action, a thought, a word? It is all of these and more. When I truly love from my heart, nothing but perfection happens. Love is like a magnet, it attracts more and more love flowing your way. The great minds speak of "loving unconditionally." When you can say "I love you" WITHOUT adding "but," "if only," "however," "yet," (you get the picture) then you have reached unconditional love. It is accepting yourself and others AS YOU/THEY ARE!

Change: Change is constant! You better believe it. You can change your clothes, your food, your exercise, your bed, your toothbrush, your car, your furniture and your mind. But the only *person* you can change is YOU. No one else – just you. The old adage: "You can lead a horse to water, but you can't make him drink" is about our expectations of change. To begin with, was the horse even thirsty? We can provide tools to others whom we sense would be better served by changing; however, it's up to them to use those tools.

Humor/Laughter: The "'coyote"– the jokester depicted in American Indian lore – reminds us to find the humor in those times when life bats us down. If you can't laugh at your mistakes, however big or small, stress will settle like a concrete mantle around your shoulders and weigh you down. I have found that laughter defuses tense situations. It releases the pressure that has been built up. There were times when I couldn't stop laughing at something ridiculous, but felt so cleansed afterward.

Regret: Nothing is worse than living your life filled with regret over choices you've made, or didn't make. It's equivalent to the "crying over spilled milk" syndrome. You have to move forward, make better choices, say what you intend, live your life fully, and know that whatever you do is OKAY! My spiritual mentor once told me, "What is right in your own eyes is what is right for you." I no longer waste time lamenting over past choices, wondering if I had done it differently where would I be now.... I can only move forward, learning from the past, knowing that those choices I sow today are the issues I will reap tomorrow.

Your Dreams/Desires: We have always encouraged you to follow your dreams, whatever they might be. Pursue them as best you can with all you possess and visualize the outcome. Learn the steps necessary to make them a reality. More than anything make sure they are YOUR dreams, not someone else's. Also, acknowledge if your dreams are "pie in the sky" or if based in real abilities (as in dreaming of becoming the world's greatest vocal artist, but you can't carry a tune). Learn what your "gifts" are and use them.

Forgive: It is in the true act of forgiveness that your spirit will be free of perceived guilt, threats, anger, judgments, fears, wrongdoings, and the list goes on. Practice the three acts of forgiveness often: Forgive yourself; forgive the situation; forgive the person whom you think caused it. It's when you "hang on" to the negative thought, act, feeling of a situation/person/yourself, that you become trapped by it and in it, so your perceptions are skewed and your choices only result in more destruction.

Health: Pay attention to your health by eating a balanced diet, exercising, and maintaining a thankful and happy attitude. Remember, what you do NOW will come back to haunt you later in life. Trust me! How many times did our good friend Wild Bill say, "If I'd known I'd live this long, I'd taken better care of myself."? You can have all of the money, fame, luck, skills, etc. in the world, but if you don't have your health, how can you enjoy it?

Abundance: Remember, what you focus on you bring to you. Too many times we focus on the lack in our lives rather than the abundance we have. Abundance comes in family, friends, work, career, home, things, or whatever. Don't to be stingy with yourself and others. Think and act abundantly.

Give Back: Share your talents with others. Volunteer at a soup kitchen, a school, or help those who are in need, or donate to your favorite charities. The world stage is shifting toward a gentler, kinder place in which to live. Be at the forefront of this change. Pay it forward!

Joy: Live in Joy! Feel the beauty of your accomplishments. Bring joy to everything you do. If you have a job/career you're not happy doing - change it. Or look at your job from a place of joyfulness and, I guarantee, it will get better.

Thankfulness: Be thankful for whatever is going on in your life. You've created it in one sense or another. The more you are thankful, the more "good things" come your way. People you interface with will resonate with your thankful attitude and you will be surprised at the blessings you'll receive.

****

Quotes and Adages I love:
"Color outside the lines."[4] – (I love this – it's creativity at its best.)

"Life is what happens to you when you're busy making other plans!"[5] – *John Lennon* – (How many times have I learned to laugh when life throws me for a loop? Too numerous to count!)

"Oh what a tangled web we weave, when first we practice to deceive"[6] – *Sir Walter Scott* – (my mother quoted this many times. Besides, lying takes too much work!)

"What goes around comes around." (Karmic Wheel)

****

A little Wisdom from your Grandmothers:
Your great-Grandma Thompson learned this from her mother: *When you go to sleep at night, look over your day and you'd BETTER have accomplished something worthwhile.* Grandma told me how much her life was influenced by it. It's good advice. Even if you "played" all day, make sure it was worthwhile.

Grandma was an avid reader who constantly reminded my brothers and me to "look it up" whenever we asked her for help in spelling or answers to some homework question. In retrospect, good advice, even though it was a pain to do it. She also embodied courage. After finding out she had that rare form of cancer called: angiosarcoma at age eighty-two, her positive and courageous outlook was truly inspiring and kept her going until her passing in 2009 at age eight-six

A Mother's Wisdom

I have been blessed to have had such a tremendous relationship with my mother-in-law, your Nana. As you know she was big on "respect" and "family." She was a wonderful example of someone who wasn't afraid to give of herself, nurture others, remain positive in adversity and love from her heart. When you decide to marry, I wish for you the same happiness I have found.

My darlings, you are greater than the sum of your parts. You are a divine being having a human experience. There is a Force, a Universal Force, of which we are a part, no matter what our ego tells us. We are connected to everything—humans, animals, and plants—all of it. This is the subtle nature of things. Because we can't always "see" the outcome of our actions, we don't realize the effect we have on ourselves and others. So, be aware of your thoughts, your actions, your words, and your feelings as they are the tools which will either heal or harm yourself and others.

I am honored to be your mother in this life experience. You are perfection in who you are, right now. I love you with a deep and abiding love. I know your lives are meant to be greater than even you can imagine.

Oh, and Vienna, Austria? A beautiful place to visit; however, I'm glad my life has turned out as it has!

Cathi - three incredible grown sons

Cathryn J. Lombardo

A Mother's Wisdom - Peggy

Strong women,
May we know them,
May we raise them,
May we be them.

*P*assion. Without it, life is boring. With it, each day has meaning and purpose: your path becomes clear.
Fear. Without it, life is filled with possibilities. With it, you may never reach your full potential.

I believe helping my children discover something to be passionate about, and teaching them not to fear success, is my greatest gift to them. As a child, I was passionate about many things, but from my parents, I learned to be overly cautious. When I started college, I chose the safety of a major in journalism rather than exploring my passions for archeology and art. Writing seemed a low-risk way to explore all of my passions, without having to zero in on a single one. But then, I started my family before finishing college, and my main focus shifted from starting a career to making sure that my daughters had the experiences they needed to become fearless and successful. My passion became helping them find the direction and strength that I had lacked as a child.

This was a fairly easy task with my first daughter. As a rather shy six-year-old, Jennifer Robin was not the sort of child I imagined might go on to become a professional actress and teacher until she owned the stage at her first ballet recital. While all of the budding ballerinas were darling, Jennifer's confidence and passion about performing were clearly something rare in a six-year-old. Watching her perform has continued to be one of my greatest joys. She gives every project her best effort and loves sharing her talent with anyone who wants to watch. Presently, as a dedicated on-camera teacher, she gives her students the same sort of training and encouragement that she was given, thereby passing on a wonderful legacy of confidence and artistic expression to another generation.

When Jennifer decided to change her college major from journalism to performing arts, like most mothers I worried about the insecurity of a professional acting career. Yet, I encouraged her to pursue her passion rather than voicing my fears. I did not want her to ever look back on her life, wondering what might have been. While another path could have been safer and more lucrative, that path might also have felt like a dead-end. I have never regretted encouraging her to take a chance on her talent; and I know that she has not regretted her choice of occupation.

Daughter number two clearly was not destined to spend her time onstage. Dana hated her first dance class and had no desire to act. From an early age, her passion was animals. She spent her childhood outdoors, collecting toads and snakes and learning about them by observation and reading. Gradually, as we adopted a menagerie of pets, she exhibited a true talent for animal psychology and training. Dana had an innate ability to elicit the behavior she wanted from our dogs and horses, as well as from most of the people she knew. She joined both dog and horse 4-H, and trained our pets to bring in the paper, play dead, and become well-behaved members of the family.

When Dana decided she did not want to finish college, I tried to persuade her to continue, but also gave her the option of a professional dog training school. She took that option, and afterward went back to college for one more year. Again, she said that finishing college was not for her, and even though I wanted to see her get a degree, I supported her in finding her own path. I knew she would find her way and that finishing college would not insure a successful life.

So, Dana became a professional dog trainer who traveled the world with her own dogs, even qualifying four times for the Schutzhund World Championships. She made a fine living training dogs, until she decided to focus on helping our family business grow. The same qualities that made her a successful animal trainer now serve her well in the world of business. She has lived her passions without fear, for which I am very thankful.

Our third daughter was not as easy to read as her sisters. With quiet confidence, Monica observed the workings of the world while she navigated successfully through school as an excellent, self-motivated student. She was good at whatever she did, and I never had to tell her, "Do your homework" or worry that she might leave college without a degree. Like Jennifer, Monica enjoyed dance class and being in plays, and like Dana, she was also dedicated to training her 4-H horse. She enjoyed some of the same activities as her sisters, yet she did not share their passion for making those activities into a career.

I believe that living in the shadow of two strong-willed older sisters taught her to get what she wanted through subtle negotiation. In high school, debate and mock trial became Monica's favorite extracurricular activities. When she later applied for law school, I knew that she had discovered her passion at her own pace, without much help from anyone else. She is now a dedicated public defender who makes a positive difference in her clients' lives, and she loves her chosen career.

As I see it, a mother's job is to meet the physical needs of her children, yet see beyond them. Our most important job is to look into their hearts and nurture their passions. Feed them healthy food, but also feed each child's spirit and encourage them to become the person they want to be--not the person *you* want them to be.

If they want to dance, make sure they get the lessons they need. If being in plays is important to them, then take them to auditions and sit though endless practices and help them balance their schoolwork with their passion.

If they are drawn to animals, adopt some. Let them learn the responsibility of caring for pets. Sign them up with activities like 4-H, where they can excel at their passion. Believe that they will find a way to make their passion work.

And, if you're not quite sure what their passion is, then trust that they will eventually find it on their own. Each of us has our own pacing. Be patient, and expose them to many things so that they will have choices. And tell them often that you know they can do whatever they set their minds to. Be a can-do fearless parent, and you will produce can-do fearless children.

Cathryn J. Lombardo

And never, never forget that mothering children is a relationship, not a job.

Peggy – three beautiful daughters; three grandchildren

A Mother's Wisdom – Julie

The most important lesson I want to teach my children is to be honest! Not only with other people, but with themselves.

I have tried to teach my children that it is important to be compassionate and help others.

Whatever you are doing in life, try your hardest to make a difference in the world.

I hope my children respect themselves and others in their life.

Don't put things off - there might not be a tomorrow.

Stand up for what you believe in.

Cathryn J. Lombardo

I have always told them they may speak freely at home, but be careful what you say around other people.

Unfortunately the world in which we live, I have to teach my children not to trust people too freely.

People will come and go in your life – remember, family comes first. Always put them first before anything else. My hope is that my children take our family traditions and use them in their families.

When you find a good friend hold on to them, keep in touch with them because true friends are hard to find.

Education is important...so go to school.

I think religion is important, but it is also important to have an open mind. Remember, we will all end up knowing the truth in the end.

Remember to enjoy the good times and try not to be preoccupied by life's worries.

A true "mother's love" is the ultimate love - it is unconditional and forever.

My mom, grandmother and grandfather taught me the lessons that made me who I am today. I hope I can pass everything they have given me down to my children.

My hope is that my children grow up to be happy and have a full life. Most important, I hope my children know and feel LOVED.

Julie – one son and one daughter

Cathryn J. Lombardo

A Mother's Wisdom

Motherhood is Survival of the Craziest

When facing my own mediocrity, I often remind myself that I have the honor, privilege, and gifted horse sense to have raised two children who are functional in society. As a young mom, I never would've believed my kids would've survived this long. If the incurable diseases hadn't gotten them, it was the other challenges that could've done them in.

After giving birth in a frantic snow storm following a ten hour work day on nothing but a packet of dry instant oatmeal, I knew my first child was destined to be strange. Taking off in his Little Tykes car on a six-lane thoroughfare, while I hobbled in my eight month pregnant state searching for him in the nearby park, was only the beginning. Soon, he was running into book cases and breaking his nose the night before school pictures, setting the kitchen table on fire after burning my candles in a pyrotechnic display, and picking up baby stingrays after almost losing his hand from a too-close encounter. This was the kid I sent to a communist country for a summer exchange student program. Was I crazy?

Although I had taken him on countless hospital visits to stitch him back together as well as many more to keep him breathing after his bouts with asthma, by the time he turned seventeen, I knew he could handle anything life threw his way, even in China. I wasn't always a believer. There were times when I'd fall to my knees in tearful, desperate prayer and ask God to help him live one more day or to see life through more logical eyes. Those were the days when I hounded my friends for advice on how to raise a child who was always one gasp away from falling off a cliff. As they watched their own docile offspring play quietly, they would smile and tell me he would grow out of it. He never did.

Tiny and wiry, my son joined Boy Scouts so he could hop over the most boulders, run into the most trees, and bring home the most pet tarantulas. In school, he demanded attention from his exhausted teachers who would ask me, time and time again, if he had been tested for ADHD. With a borderline diagnosis, all I could do was to eliminate his sugar intake and keep him busy. Basketball and soccer worked for a while, along with science camps and invention conventions, but the school principal knew him far too well for my comfort.

Through all this, I dragged my gastric-challenged daughter back and forth, mopping up her vomit along the way. By the time she was three, we had her gastroenterologist on speed dial. Miserable and constantly being strapped into a car seat, she put up with me racing her brother to various and sundry activities in an attempt to keep him busy as well as current with his allergy and counseling specialists.

By sixth grade, my energetic but tortured son announced he needed a change from his current educational institution. We went shopping and discovered the wonderful world of Socratic learning. Although the special charter school boasted four hours of homework a night through a strict academic regimen, the idea of being able to discuss his ideas in class so enthralled the kid he promised he'd never complain about school again.

After two tearful years of effort, my son snapped out of his funk. He came home bursting with interesting tidbits from class. Pouring over his books at night, he emerged tired but confident he did his best. The bullies were still there – nerds can be tormentors, too – but he worked through his challenges without making it on the headmaster's hit list. Wonder of wonders, my son was maturing. He joined the speech and debate team, co-led the Latin club's spring convention, and became an Eagle Scout. In his spare time, he created musical instruments, wildly inventive drawings, and began shaping his hopes and dreams.

Cathryn J. Lombardo

Through all this, my daughter was diagnosed with acid reflux disease and put on a strict regimen of pills and special food. The easy part was finding out how to keep her out of the hospital. Once she managed to keep food inside her, she became the opposite of her brother and blossomed into a young, mature woman far ahead of her peers. Constant taunting and nude cartoon pictures of her voluptuous development circulated throughout the elementary boys' circles. We cried together, not only over the boys' cruelty, but the hatred and jealousy of her girlfriends as well. Patient and kind, she suffered for years as she searched for confidantes she could trust. By high school, my beautiful girl became extremely vociferous and depressed. Finally turning to acting, writing, and dance, she found the outlets and confidence she needed to build lasting friendships.

My children now face a far more daunting prospect than permanent hospitalization or becoming the school pariah. With calls from Dartmouth and Vanderbilt alumni for interviews, my son will soon be leaving for college. A new set of worries besets me. He can drive a car and even talk himself down from a panic attack, but can he handle the pseudo-adult world of a university? Will he be the one who drinks the most beers in one night, or will he discover a new quasar telescope? I worry about my daughter losing her older sibling as well. The less clingy of my two children, she never had much use for me when it came to advice. After all, what would I, a bumbling geek who didn't have a best friend until college, know about social issues? Just as her brother worked through his own social challenges, he helped her do the same through whacky antics of running up to her at her locker to give her a noogie when she looked her lowest or plop a duct tape hat he made on her head. Although I have become as nutty as her brother, I doubt there will ever be a time when I get a laugh out of her. I am just not cool enough.

With the confident survival of my two children, I know my molding and teaching days are pretty much done. Soon, I will no longer tell them to have fun storming the castle when they leave for school in the morning. They will be steering their own futures while I watch and support. With my innate need to hit the brakes and serve as a safety net, this will be far tougher for me than it will for them. I have already told myself I will not cry over my son's empty bedroom and the lack of raucous laughter reverberating throughout the house. I will not sleep with my daughter's ballet slippers under my pillow and wish she was a little girl again. I will send them gifts instead, and perhaps show up on their doorsteps when they least expect it, bearing a tray of cookies they love and the cabbage soup they loathe. After all, they can't have everything.

Most of all, I will get on with my life. Thanks to my children, I have been forced out of my shell to face adversity with zaniness and hope. I gave up my quiet home business and any chance at a full-time job when I focused on my children's needs, but the flight of my two nestlings has only made me feel more useful. Like the Giving Tree who has lost everything but her trunk, I will still offer an ear to listen and a place to regroup, as well as sprout new branches so I can start anew. Motherhood has shown me I may be crazy, but I am not mediocre at all. I have raised two promising, healthy people who will join me in watching our fabulous futures as they come to fruition together.

Stacey – one son and one daughter

A Mother's Wisdom

From the Journal of Gypsy Le Fai

Life is a journey.
Follow the flow.
Pay attention to the signs.
Listen to your heart.
Embrace your dreams.

If your dreams see signs, follow your heart. If your heart sees signs, follow your dreams. And, when the two are one, you'll know that you are on the right path.

Stuff

Stuff; be it emotional or material, it is the weight of the world. *Stuff* is a negative source interrupting the flow of energy. In order to be free and live above the *stuff*, we need to be as light as we can be. Set the *stuff* aside and be free.

Choices
Our journey consists of parallel pathways. Each will take you where you are to go, just differently. Make conscious decisions along the way.

"Womanifest"
A new word derived from "manifest". Its definition – When a *woman* manifests her dreams.

Hell
The hell to be endured, the hereafter of which theology tells, is no worse than the hell we make for ourselves in this world by habitually fashioning ourselves in the wrong way. We spin our own fate, good and evil.

Now
Stay focused on the moment. Let go of the past. Don't worry about the future.

Willingness: (Quotes)
"There is nothing more powerful than an idea whose time has come."[7] – *Victor Hugo*

"In order to eliminate the negative influences, simply ignore them."[8] – Lao-*tzu*

Affirmations
You are entitled to be respected, loved, and happy; to feel fulfilled and prosperous; to enjoy all of the moments of your

life. Do whatever it takes to fulfill your dreams, and you have the luxury of NOT needing to explain your actions to anyone.

Power
Never underestimate the power to change yourself.
Never overestimate your power to change others.

Excuses
Who would you be if you never had anyone telling you who you are? You can never change the actions of others, you can only change yourself.

Gentleness
When you have the choice to be right or to be kind, always be kind. Gentleness implies that you no longer need to dominate or control others. When you have developed this virtue, the pronoun "I" ceases to be the center of your communication. Beginning a sentence with "I" implies the need to control. Gentleness means accepting life and people as they are, rather than insisting that they be as *you* are.

Happiness
Happiness is a state of mind, a state of consciousness that we can develop, feel, and appreciate – like faith. A happy state of mind moves us into successful experiences.

Cathryn J. Lombardo

Imagination

Imagination is the engineering part of our mind. Through our imagination, our desires are fulfilled. We automatically move toward what we imagine.

My Daughters

Daughter - at birth you were dedicated to God. When you need guidance, go within and listen to your heart's spirit. That place is your direct connection to God. You can trust that place for your truth.

Gypsy – three beautiful daughters; four wonderful grandsons and one delightful granddaughter; and dog, Pepper

A Mother's Wisdom – Jackie

Thinking about the wisdom I would share with my children, two wonderful young men, depends on the day, the circumstances and the situation. Thinking over the twenty-four years I have spent as a mother has made me realize that there were very few conversations that began with the intention of imparting "wisdom" to my children.

As boys become men, you get a glimpse of what you have helped to shape. I say that with some reservation as I think of my boys as being strong and unique individuals, but as I know my parents shaped me, I see that I too have helped to shape my sons.

To have a strong sense of love and loyalty to the family was something I hoped, more than anything that my boys would have, especially to one another. I knew that they had developed this with two memorable Mother's Day gifts.

Cathryn J. Lombardo

The first came when Mick was attending Santa Clara University in the Bay Area. Dean, a high school senior, went to visit Mick over Mother's Day weekend. We sent Dean once a year to spend time with Mick and they made their annual trip to China Town. This particular year, Dean came back on the plane with a long narrow object which he handed to me at the baggage claim, announcing, "Happy Mother's Day!" The boys had picked up a Samurai sword because they were always joking that they were going to buy swords and go fight out in the backyard. But the part that really hugged my heart was when they explained the care they took until they found the perfect one. They wanted me to display it, and figured it would go best in the dining room. They knew I wouldn't display it unless it matched, so they found a beautiful sword in a white case, matching my blue and white plates. And yes, I have the sword proudly displayed in the dining room.

The following year, as Mick was finishing University, Dean joined his brother in the Bay area where he was attending Berkeley. This time, the gift came as a telephone call. The boys actually did not see each other very often that year as neither had a car and the Cal train was two hours one way. Mother's Day morning, Dean was first on the phone. "Mick and I are here to wish you a Happy Mother's Day," he said. "Where are you two?" I asked. They went on to tell me that they were spending the weekend together, because they knew that it was so important to me that they remain close. And they couldn't think of anything that would make me happier than knowing that they were spending time together.

Love and loyalty. They had gotten the message.
Do I have wisdom? I think I do. A wisdom shared by all mothers.

Jackie – two grown sons

Cathryn J. Lombardo

A Mother's Wisdom

For Ian

The day I learned my essay would be included in *A Mother's Wisdom*, I panicked! My essays are all about events in my life close to my heart. Mostly, they're for writers or anyone who has a passion for something close to theirs. But this time, I had the chance to write an essay for you. To guide you as you take one of life's big steps. I didn't know where to begin. I brainstormed a lot and wrote a little. There were many false starts and lots of frustration. Until finally, I put the essay away to work on something else.

The ideas and words percolated in my mind as I went through my week. I thought about the past and I thought about your future. And when I sat at the computer once again, the words came a little easier. Soon you'll be leaving for college. Off to a new and exciting life and the beginning of something wonderful. Now, as I sit in my chair in the office and flip through the pages of the calendar to August, the day seems so far away. But I know it will happen in an instant.

The years from Kindergarten to high school sped by. I remember the night before your first day of school, I told your dad, "Ian's going to be in Kindergarten. And before you know it, he'll be in middle school then high school then he'll be graduating from college." I'm sure the words tumbled out of my mouth practically on top of each other. But really, your entire future was racing through my mind. Dad laughed and said, "Honey, you have him starting elementary school and graduating from college in all of about one minute."

You know what? Sometimes, the thirteen years from your first day of school to almost your last seem to have gone by in just about sixty seconds. And I'm sure the college years will speed by at an even faster clip. The day you leave won't be easy for us; and I bet it won't be easy for you either.

So how can I help make the transition from high school to life as a college student a little easier? I'll begin by saying Dad and I believe in you. We know that whatever you want to do in life... *You can succeed!*

See the Forest and the Trees
It's as easy as - seeing the forest *and* the trees. This is my twist on an old saying, referring to someone who isn't able to see the whole picture because he's focusing too much on the little

things. Or maybe, worrying too much about how he's going to get where he's going. To see the forest and the trees, you have to be able to know where you're going and how you're going to get there. You have to set goals and do what you can to meet them. When you look ahead to a goal seemingly unattainable, chop it into smaller parts. Pieces that are not so scary to achieve. I'll be honest with you; it isn't always going to be easy. But that's okay, nothing worthwhile is ever effortless. You might know the feeling already. After a long summer working in Bristol Bay with Dad and the other crewmembers, you finally got to put the boat away and look back to see what you've all accomplished. I've seen your smiles and heard your stories and I know it's worthy of celebrating. Especially when you can celebrate among friends.

Don't Surround Yourself with Yourself

The words from the song: *"I've Seen All Good People"*[9] - from the band, *Yes* are floating around in my mind. I loved listening to you and Dad sing and I'll remember those times forever. The song's lyrics "Don't surround yourself with yourself" are forever contemporary and insightful. A solo voice, accompanied by only a mandolin and the beat of a drum is soon joined by others. As the voices blend into a beautiful harmony, the sound of flutes and an electric piano surround them. Words and an amazing medley are woven together. By the end of the song, you can't help but smile. Life is the same way. People need each other! Though it's true you need to rely on yourself as you go through life, it's also true you don't always need to go it alone. There are times you're going to need help. Gather your friends and family around you. Don't be afraid to ask for help and don't be afraid to listen. Sounds simple, but it isn't always easy. Especially when your mind is racing in a million different directions at once.

Keep Your Nose Clean
Pop-Pop constantly reminded us to "Keep your nose clean." I always loved when he said stuff like that. Even when I was little, I knew he had been talking about more than a spot of dirt on my nose. He'd been telling me, as well as your aunts and uncles, to "stay out of trouble." It didn't matter where we were going or who we might be with, he'd always say, "Keep your nose clean" before we headed out the door. And, before I made a decision, or did something stupid, his words filtered into my mind. I still hold fast to his guidance. Looking back, I think those words are one of the smartest pieces of advice he's ever given me.

Let Things Simmer
I have one more suggestion before I let you go. Please remember to let things simmer. There will be times in life when you're going to have to make some pretty tough decisions. Choices you imagine you can't make. Maybe lots of different ideas will hit you at once. Or maybe nothing will hit you. If it's not an emergency, really, it's okay to think about them. Take the time to consider every option. Write your thoughts down, let them bubble and then decide the best

course of action. Like the words in my essay, the resolution will come a little easier. Of course you won't always have the luxury of waiting. When that happens, use the good intuition I know you have and make the decision. If you're making it with the best intentions, it will be the right one.

We're all proud of you, Ian. And I know we are all looking forward to seeing the man you'll become. So, as you graduate and head off to college, remember, "Keep your nose clean" and have fun!

Love Mom

Donna – one son

Cathryn J. Lombardo

A Mother's Wisdom

My Family's Particular Wisdom

I would like to mention that I happen to be the best housekeeper in my maternal family line. Before that sounds impressive, I have to also mention that my family, generation after generation, are a group hoarders like you wouldn't believe. My family is inordinately fond of plastic bags, and will save them to the level of slapstick humor. Throwing out a plastic bag is literally cause for a call to the nice people at the Suicide Hotline for my family.

We're also "pilers," meaning we have stacks of stuff all over the place on any flat or semi-flat surface. We can all find whatever "it" is we're looking for in the stacks, and if not, it clearly wasn't important, so what the heck, right? If we can't find it, it probably wasn't important anyway, is how we live our lives. Sure, that means we get some fun calls and visits due to ignoring key pieces of mail like jury summons or lawyers' notes, but overall, it's worked like a charm, decade after decade.

When I went away to college I learned that there were people, nay, whole groups of citizens, who didn't hoard *or* pile. Imagine my surprise. These folks cleaned on a regular basis, too. And not just surface "what you can see with the naked eye at a quick glance in a dimly lit room" cleaning, but deep down, *under* the collectibles and books cleaning. Color me shocked to my core.

So, when I got married, I decided we'd do things a little differently. Oh, sure, I hoard the plastic bags -- it's a family tradition, after all -- but only until they overflow their small section in my pantry. Yes, "overflow" is a subjective term, but if the door cannot close, some bags go.

I still pile, but less than any others with my genetic strain and also with the semi-regular habit of actually lessening the piles and putting things in their place. So, for my family, I'm a cleaning *whiz*.

However, there is one huge piece of cleaning wisdom that's been carefully handed down from mother to daughter for generations, which I follow to the letter. As such, I want to be sure it doesn't get lost to the world. I've already passed it along to my daughter, and she's learned it well, so I now give it to you freely. No need to thank me -- that's just the kind of girl I am.

In every domicile in which you live, be it a postage stamp-sized apartment or the Taj Mahal, there must be a closet near the front door. And it is in this closet that the vacuum cleaner lives. You can put anything else you want into the closet, but nothing can block the vacuum cleaner's easy and unhindered access.

This is so, when the doorbell rings unexpectedly, you can go to the closet, open the closet door, pull out the vacuum cleaner, close the closet door, and then open your front door in one fluid series of movements. Then you say, to whomever happens to be standing there -- best friend, random door-to-door salesman, Jehovah's Witness, federal marshal -- "Oh! I was just getting ready to clean! You can come in, but the house is a mess. Better yet, let's go out! Hang on a moment and I'll grab my purse."

Then, once you're back from lunch, spending money, hearing the Word, or visiting the police lineup, you open the closet door, put the vacuum cleaner back into the closet, and close the closet door. Then you are free to go on about your life.

Note that at no time whatsoever is the vacuum cleaner ever turned *on*. I grew up thinking they were a lifetime item. We used the vacuum cleaner about twice a year. When the one I'd grown up and turned into an older teenager with finally coughed and died a noble death, I cried. Then we got a wet/dry vac, one that didn't need one of those silly bags to mess with and could be used for years without needing emptying. I loved it like a brother.

When my husband and I got married, most of our wedding party, knowing my prowess with housekeeping, chipped in and got us a vacuum cleaner. They mentioned to the hubs that they'd gotten the best that Sears made and they kindly told me that I'd get used to the noise one day, and they all stressed that this was going to die and then the hubs would, for some reason, demand that we buy another.

One male member of our wedding party did not go in on the vacuum cleaner. He gave us a color TV. He was a bit embarrassed, because he'd bought it with his credit card frequent user bucks, but we didn't care. It was a color TV and not a major cleaning appliance. We didn't own either before our marriage, and I can say for me, at least, that TV was far more fun and entertainment than the vacuum cleaner ever was. The TV lasted a lot longer, too.

We are on our fifth or sixth vacuum cleaner in our marriage now. We've given our daughter a vacuum cleaner, too. And when we helped her find her apartment, I ensured she had a coat closet right by the front door. I also stressed that she should always remember our family's Secret Phrase, which she assures me she had memorized long before she moved out.

I have more wisdom, but we're out of space. Feel free to drop by if you want to get more tips like this to make your lives better. I'd be happy to invite you in, but I was just getting ready to clean...

Jeanne – one daughter

(Originally published in part as "Fur Schway" at Raphael's Village, http://www.raphaelsvillage.com)

Cathryn J. Lombardo

My Gift to My Grandchildren

How often have we said, "If I could only do it over, I'd do it differently?" Unfortunately, most of us don't get that opportunity, but what we can do is pass on what we've learned from our life experiences to the next generation. In my case, the next generation has now become the next-next generation. My granddaughter is pregnant, and I want her and my great grandchildren to have what I wasn't always wise enough to give to my children. So this is what I've learned as a parent, grandparent, teacher and observer of life.

1. Life is not about you anymore. Your child's needs come before your own.
2. With that being said, make time for yourself every day. If you give every moment of every day to your children, spouse, friends, and/or job, you will lose a part of your

SELF. If you're happy, chances are everyone else will be happy, too.
3. Make time for you and your spouse. A happy, healthy relationship can get you through those tough times, and there will be many.
4. Agree before you start a family as to how you and your spouse want to raise and discipline your children. Be united in your decisions! Kids know when you don't agree and will play you against each other.
5. Don't make threats you are not willing to carry out. Your kids will call your bluff, and you'll look the fool.
6. Use a soft, firm voice when disciplining – don't yell and don't argue!!
7. Don't overuse the word NO. If possible think your decision through before answering. Sometimes NO becomes an automatic response, especially when you're busy, tired, or frustrated, and the decision is made in haste.
8. When they're young and they get into EVERYTHING, distract them. Give them a positive alternative.
9. Tell your children you're proud of them; they can't hear it enough.
10. Learn to budget your money!!!!! If you want something and don't have the money for it, save up for it.

A Mother's Wisdom

11. Don't give your children everything they want. Teach them to save up their allowance for what they want.
12. Give them chores to do at an early age. They can start by cleaning up their toys - make it a game. Give them more responsibility as they get older; it teaches them to be accountable and self-reliant.
13. Be positive! Negativity creates negativity and a poor self-esteem.
14. School is the first priority, but make sure to involve them in extracurricular activities. Just don't make the extracurricular activity their life.
15. Admit when you're wrong and say you're sorry; kids need to know that adults are not perfect.
16. Be consistent, but on the other hand, don't be too rigid.
17. Spend time with your kids – it doesn't have to cost money, e.g. play games, go for a walk, go to the park, read.
18. Read to them! Read to them! *Read to them!* Even when they are old enough to read, take turns reading to each other.
19. Don't try to solve everything for them. Let them stumble and fall – that's a part of life! Better to learn life's lessons early rather than when they're older and the consequences could be more severe.

20. Never talk negatively about the other parent within hearing distance of your children. Even if you don't think they're listening, they are.
21. Teach them to problem solve. We are very busy and sometimes it's easier to just do "it" for them, but in the long run, we're not doing them any favors. Ask them what steps they have taken to solve their problem before they asked you for help.
22. Life is not fair! Sometimes you lose! Teach them to lose gracefully.
23. It's okay to make a mistake because it's only a mistake if you don't learn a valuable lesson from it.
24. Expose your children to a variety of culture, nature, etc. It adds to their overall well-being.
25. If you are really angry, it's okay to take a time-out for both of you. It will prevent you from over reacting and doing something you will later regret.
26. Kids will argue with you. It's their inherent nature. It's very trying for you, but it's proof they're growing up. They are only trying to become more independent.
27. Be patient! Learn to count to 10, 20, 30.........
28. Know what's normal for any given age. It relieves some of the stress knowing that your kids are normal and not little psychos in the making.

29. Let them make some of their own decisions, even at a young age. It makes them feel you respect their opinions.
30. Do everything with love!
31. Homework should be done in a quiet place with few distractions.
32. Teach them how to organize themselves so time is spent wisely.
33. Make a calendar for the whole family of weekly obligations, e.g. appointments, homework, long-term assignments, extracurricular activities.
34. Check their homework.
35. Meet the parents of your children's friends.
36. Check up on your kids. Know where they are at all times and with whom.
37. If your gut tells you something isn't right, it probably isn't.
38. Remember you are their parent, not their friend.
39. Eat healthy! It is true you are what you eat. Ask yourself if your child's brain will like what they're eating. We all want smart kids.
40. Life does not always turn out the way we want it to turn out.
41. If you stay out late, remember your kids are still going to get up at the same time they usually do. Don't take it

out on them if you're tired, they won't leave you alone, they're too loud, and/or they constantly want your attention.
42. Show your kids how important exercise is by setting an example and make it fun for them to participate.
43. Limit their time in front of the TV, video games, and computer. Make them go outside and play.
44. Don't put a computer in their bedroom and always monitor their time and use on it.
45. Be a positive role model!
46. Watch your potty mouth!!!
47. It's okay to disagree with your spouse but don't yell and scream at each other in front of the kids - work it out through discussion. It's good for kids to see how problems are solved. If you're really angry, have your discussion behind closed doors but remember you can hear through walls and vents.
48. Talk, read, and sing to your baby while you're pregnant.
49. Designate one day a week for family time. Take turns choosing an activity.
50. Teach your child how to cook. Let them be in charge of one meal per week.
51. Think positive!! Always look for the good in any given situation and vocalize it.

A Mother's Wisdom

52. Let your children see you being affectionate with your spouse, G-rated, of course.
53. Involve kids in family decisions.
54. Eat at the kitchen table without the TV on. It's a great time to catch up on each other's lives.
55. If you want respect, treat your children with respect.
56. Don't call your child names; it's disrespectful!
57. Hugs are free! Give them freely and often.
58. Your children are gifts from God. Treat them as such.

AND

59. Tell them you love them every single day.

They say that with age comes wisdom, so hopefully these words of wisdom will help you to be a better parent than I was. (For Kylee: Enjoy this incredible journey of parenthood.)

Love,
Mema

Lynda – one daughter and one son; four grandchildren; one soon-to-be great-grand child

Cathryn J. Lombardo

A Mother's Wisdom

A Mother's Advice

I remember a profound sentence spoken light-heartedly by a priest/counselor/friend years ago when I was whining in his office. He smiled warmly and shook his head slightly as he said tenderly, "We take ourselves so seriously."

I think of it from time to time when I'm smarting from a disappointment, even a small one, like a clerk in a store speaking rudely to me. I've learned that one's feelings follow one's beliefs, and if we can find that belief we can choose to change it if we want to. My mistaken belief is, "People should always be nice to me if I'm nice to them." Nice as that would be, not everyone thinks that way. Rather than expect them to change their beliefs and behavior, I can change only mine to "People will not always be nice to me, and I can stand that."

We can "give them permission," (not verbally, but in our minds) to act any way they want, short of abusing us physically or verbally. We don't have to like their treatment, but we can remain comfortable and happy in spite of it. WE are in charge of our feelings. THEY aren't. We get to enjoy our power over our feelings and recognize our options. I don't have to become a wimpy doormat. I can be nicely assertive, which is quite different from being aggressive. Assertiveness just defines our feelings, where aggressiveness tries to control someone.

I have ever so many choices of how to respond to a testy clerk (neighbor, co-worker, relative, spouse) the first being not to respond at all but keep my equanimity and stay placid. Or I might want to say, "You bitch! You have no right to give me that disgusted look. I'll report you to your manager." I might even stick out my tongue at her if that would make me feel better. I could laugh at her. I could even say something sympathetic, like, "It must have been a difficult morning for you."

However I choose to act, I want it to be what makes me the most comfortable. I like being able to think, "Humph. What an unhappy woman she is. I'm glad I'm not," and walk away, pleased with my purchase rather than being distraught. I know from experience that losing my temper gives me a rush of adrenaline that lasts longer than it needs to, leaving my heart pounding and my mind reeling. It can put a damper on my entire day and temporarily upset my life. Is it worth it? Not to me.

My job is to take back my power rather than give it to others. If I'm in charge of my mind, my beliefs and therefore my feelings, nobody else has power over me. Of course, in life others DO have power over me, like police who can fine me for speeding. But I have the power not to speed in the first place. Husbands and wives, girlfriends and boyfriends don't have power over us unless we give it to them, which I would absolutely discourage!

What we want to strive for in every relationship is mutual respect. I must respect myself, but I must also respect you. You must respect yourself and respect me. If those four rules are being honored, we can have a great relationship. If one or more of them isn't, we're in trouble.

Taking ourselves less seriously (being able to laugh at ourselves) and minding the rules of mutual respect will make any relationship much easier to manage, enabling all parties involved to enjoy life more fully.

Lee – two daughters and two sons; three grandchildren

Cathryn J. Lombardo

A Mother's Wisdom – Valeria

I have loved having two daughters; the process of raising them taught me a lot about myself and life. I have had to face parts of myself in them, which can be a growing experience for me. I also have the blessing of a wonderful relationship with each daughter. I have always emphasized with them the importance of knowing their heart and following their passions. They are both currently in college and, as they find their way in life, it is fascinating to me to see what paths they go down and the journey which leads them along.

These are a few of my personal guidelines for life and business:

Do what you say you are going to do. If I did not like what my daughters were doing, I got up and did something about it. They could count on the fact that if I said no or yes, I meant it and action would follow my words. This did not mean I never changed my mind or had a new idea, but then I would say so. I was very careful not to ever threaten any punishment or reward I could not follow through on. Frequently, I found that a creative carrot and stick combination worked well if I wanted something as onerous as room cleaning done. I would have both a reward for doing it and a negative for not cleaning the room. Like they could have a party if it was done and would be grounded if not done.

Tell the truth. When you tell the truth, you reduce the amount of information you have to remember. There is no need to think about what you have told to whom. In addition, people instinctively recognize you as a person of integrity. I have had situations where the story of what has happened to me must stretch my credibility with a stranger, but they believe me anyway. I think this is because, although I certainly do not tell everybody everything, I rarely tell even small lies.

Understand your business. Know your health, finances, property, car or home as well as anyone else does, so you are sure you are getting accurate information about repairs, management, upkeep and other aspects of your business. It is good to delegate but do it wisely, so you both respect what others are doing for you and are not taken advantage of. You have to look out for yourself and your belongings.

Treat everyone with respect and how you would like to be treated. Be aware that someone doing work for you today could someday be in a very different position in which you might work for them; or need their recommendation to get the job you want.

Do not make decisions from a place of fear. Some of the worst decisions are made based on fear, and usually not based on understanding all of the options. Move to a place of calm, balance and clarity to make the big decisions of life. Open your mind to recognize as many of your choices as you can before you narrow in on the best ones. Understand the best and worst that could happen with each option. Don't be afraid of taking a risk if the possible gain is great and the worst is manageable.

Begin with the end in mind. When my daughters were young I thought about how I wanted them to be independent women some day. So, when they went through the "NO" phase at two years old, I recognized it as the first step for them to being able to leave home someday. I encouraged them to learn life skills like doing laundry, cooking and cleaning. They received their clothes money for back-to-school shopping in a lump sum and I would drive them around to make their choices. When it was time for them to go away to college, it was still tough, but they knew how to make decisions, take risks wisely, and say no.

Understand the rules of the game. It is not always necessary to follow the rules, but it is very important to understand them. When you understand them, then you know the consequences of breaking rules and why they were established in the first place. There are rules that are arbitrary and ones that make sense in some settings but not others. Some rules are important to follow for the safety of everyone including yourself, while others are based on incomplete information. Following rules slavishly can be as dangerous as totally disregarding them. For example, I always follow the speed limit in town because of unpredictable pedestrians, other drivers, and congestion, but on the highway I may speed if traffic is light and the weather good.

These are some of my basic guidelines for my personal and professional life. They have stood me in good stead, and I hope my daughters have learned these from watching me live my life. I trust they will build on them as they create their lives.

Valeria – two daughters

A Mother's Wisdom

Children Are Hilarious

My darling adults, as you venture into marriages and the considerations of parenthood, I want to share one of my more delightful discoveries in my own parenting journey: children are hilarious. Do you remember? Let me prod your memory:

> *"Sister hit me!"*
> *"What did you do to make her mad?"* I asked the tattling four-year-old.
> *"I don't want to talk... My throat has tonsils."*

Good times.

Children have unique perspectives on the world. For example, one three-year-old daughter was watching her father coach a high school freshmen football game. The team wore white helmets and pants, and royal blue jerseys. She looked at me, eyes wide with excitement. Grinning with joy, she pointed at the players.

"*Smurfs!*" she squealed.

Yep. That is *exactly* what they looked like.

What about the dangers of over-eating? The wisdom of another's three-year old moment:

> "*If I eat too much, my stomach will pop, my arms will pop, my legs will pop... and I'll be all skinnied-up, like thread.*"

(Oh, if only that one was true.)

How about "Putting on a Show," a common childhood pursuit? Second daughter was in second grade when she created a 3-act play to be staged with her friends in our garage and video-taped. This was in the pre-computer-typewriter era, so her invitations and costuming instructions had to be painstakingly typed one by one. The first one was pretty complete and detailed. But the last one merely said:

> "*I'm putting on a play. Tell your mom to buy you a puffy dress.*"

Of course, I included an explanation for the baffled parent. The play was successfully staged with a cast of four. Five were invited, but one beautifully costumed princess refused to say her lines, burst into tears, and walked away in the throes of stage fright. Fourth-grade sister saved the day by playing multiple roles. The video is hilarious.

Speaking of older sister, she was enjoying pizza one suppertime when she pointed to her slice and asked,

> *"What is that?"*
> *"A caraway seed,"* I said.
> She gave me a horrified look. *"Pizza has seeds?"*
> (Again, if *only*...)

Sometimes, the funniest things are also the most sincere. I took my son with me, at age three, to visit a friend an hour's flight away. He carried onto the plane his own Little Tykes toy airplane, which I thought was adorable. It wasn't until he looked at me in somber seriousness and explained that I understood his reasoning:

> *"I brought this airplane in case the pilot needs another one."*

How precious is that?

Our youngest daughter always had to stand up for herself, even when it meant defying her older brother. When he, at the foolish age of three-and-a-half, took one of her toys, my little wisp of a two-year-old full-body tackled him to the ground to get it back. She left him in tears. Dad, a.k.a. the Football Coach, was never so proud.

Then there was "The Powder Incident." Son was a few months past two years old. Ten-month-old baby sister, who shared his room, was still in a crib. The two of them seemed to be waking up unusually late that morning. No sound came from their room. I carefully opened the bedroom door. Son stood in the middle of the room, covered from hair to pajama feet in baby powder. (Caldesene. Yeah, the expensive stuff.) Sister was dusted with her share as well; she rocked from foot to foot, grinning, in her crib. Son had the open tube of Desitin in his fist. He had started the smearage.

"Stay right there!" I ordered. *"Don't you dare move!"*

Then I ran and got the camera. *Priceless.*

Being a parent is never easy, not if you do it right. And while the special moments, moments like rocking your sleeping child, enjoying their first real Christmas, or greeting them after their first day of school are memorable, it's the unexpected bits that we remember the most. Those are the moments that make life real.
That make life interesting.
That make us laugh.

Daughter number two was poking around in the pantry when she turned to me, obviously disturbed. She pointed to a jar.

"Hearts?"
"Artichoke hearts," I clarified.

A Mother's Wisdom

She appeared equal parts disgusted and afraid. *"What kind of animal is an artichoke?"*

Yep. Children are hilarious.

Kris – three beautiful daughters and one studly son

Cathryn J. Lombardo

My Dearest Babies

It's funny when you are growing up through the years, you don't realize how much a mother worries about you verses the world. I worry and pray for you daily. Will you be hurt, will you make good decisions, and will you think I made good decisions raising you? There is so much for a mother to worry about. So, I would like to write some wisdom that I have struggled with in my life in hopes they may make your life a little easier.

When you were babies I acknowledged the blessing and gifts that you were, and I made a promise to raise you the best I could with your highest good in my heart. With that said, I want you to always listen to your higher self. Take quite time to reflect and just listen. Don't let your days blend together with chaos; take a moment each day to reflect. Whether it is in the shower or when you are laying down before you sleep at night, listen to your higher self and let it guide you to where your journey needs to go.

Listen to what is true and what is right. Don't fall to what the world thinks you should be doing or where they think you need to go, rather listen to your truth. Don't ever steer from your truth.

Set goals. Don't be afraid of what may happen tomorrow or the event of yesterday, it's a waste of your energy.

Live each day to the fullest as the gift it is and embrace it. Know that you cannot control the events or people around you, but you can control how you respond.

Think before you react. The saying I use all the time, "You can catch more bees with honey,"[10] is true.

Love everyone. What makes the world a better place is LOVE. If people are unkind (and they will be from time to time) you can remove yourself from them but still love them.

 Be kind to people. Even though the majority of people may think a certain way or pick on a certain person, you will come across in a better way if you are kind.

I want the two of you to be true to what you believe; don't fall to peer-pressure of what everyone else is doing. Stand up for what you believe and know that you are the better person for it.

Spend more time listening and less time talking. Know that it is not all about you, and it is our job to give back. Give to others always for the blessings you receive; you also need to give those blessings to other people.

When you were babies, I acknowledged the blessings and gifts you two are; and know that God will never leave you.

For everything you do, pray. Pray for the blessings you received and give thanks; pray for the battles you will face; pray for your friend in need; pray, pray, pray.

Lastly, in your life people will hurt you, make you angry, and be unkind - learn to let that go. Don't let it build up inside of you because it will eat you from the inside out. Give it to God, and know that the person has a lesson to learn, and you were a tool that was in place for them to learn it. And know you will be the person learning a lesson sometimes, so do everything with love. I love you both with all of my being, and am so proud of the little men you have already become.

To your journey!!

Mom

Abby – two young sons

Cathryn J. Lombardo

A Mother's Wisdom

Stubbornness as a Virtue

Kids' personality traits are hardwired. Before I had children, I believed the role of a parent was to help mold their children into successful adults. I thought if I spent enough time with my children, they would love music, or be great athletes, or great scholars. I even thought I could teach a child to be cheerful.

How naïve of me.

The grandmother who provided childcare while I taught school, pronounced my son to be the most stubborn child she'd ever cared for in the three decades she'd run her business. Every day when I picked up Dave, he was cheerfully sitting in the "time out" hallway. He wasn't resentful. I was always greeted with a cheerful, "Hi Mom," when I walked in the door.

For years, I thought this stubbornness trait would interfere with his being successful. Now, my advice to my children is to embrace those "hardwired" personality traits.

In 2001, when my son was a junior in college, he was driving with his roommate across an isolated part of Northern Arizona on the way to Moab, Utah to spend Easter vacation. At two in the morning, an oncoming car came across the centerline causing a horrendous accident.

The phone call on that (not so) "Good Friday" the Thirteenth is the one that every parent fears. Dave almost lost his life. A broken back needed rods and pins; a broken and dislocated foot was in danger of being amputated. He also had a broken jaw and missing teeth, broken ribs and punctured lung, broken nose, loss of hand motion, deep facial cuts needing plastic surgery, skewed vision which would require multiple surgeries, and traumatic brain injury. In three months, he had over thirty-five doctors in three hospitals. I will never forget driving to Farmington, New Mexico and walking into his room in ICU to see over thirty wires and tubes connected to his body.

The nurses were concerned because he wouldn't respond to anybody. I walked in, took his hand and said, "Mommy is here. Squeeze my hand if you love your mom." The squeeze crushed my fingers. We knew his brain worked.

A Mother's Wisdom

It became apparent to all of Dave's family that the key to his success was his stubbornness. He never gave up on his recovery as he learned to walk and train his brain. He started Arizona State University that fall, living alone in an apartment and unable to drive. That first semester, he was in a body brace and in a wheelchair, and rode the bus over two hours each way to travel just two miles to one class. The University's security would meet him with a golf cart at the bus station and take him to his classes. This was only four months after the accident! My son never missed a class, made up all his incomplete classes, and graduated with a degree in elementary education.

I was sure any healthy college student facing a similar accident would do everything possible to recover. Then my neighbor survived a motorcycle accident with injuries similar to my son's. This young man would only do therapy if his mother bribed him with cigarettes. The doctors thought he might walk, but he didn't try. Although capable, he refused to take care of his personal hygiene for several years. His family will never know how much he could have improved.

Dave still sees double in the bottom half of his vision field. I always felt he should be paid twice as much as a teacher because, when he looks down, his class size is doubled. After several partially successful eye surgeries by a neuro-opthamologist, he compensates by tipping his head down so he can clearly see to drive and read. He wears a foot brace and walks in constant pain.

One year after the accident, he climbed half a mile to an Eco-lodge on La Isla Del Sol in Lake Titicaca, Peru. Llamas hauled his luggage, while his sister and uncle supported him under each shoulder on the hike back down to the boat. Two years after the accident, I watched him hike and hunt in the rugged Southern Arizona terrain even though he could not look down and clearly see where to put his feet, and every rolling rock underfoot was agony. He took a community college guitar class to regain better control of his right hand, but now compensates activities with his left hand, because the right didn't recover completely. Of course he sets off metal detectors with all his plates, rods and pins. In spite of his accident, I defy anyone to realize he is handicapped.

My son is my hero for never giving up. He refused to take antidepressants because he did not want to change his personality. He refused to get his ankle fused in case he could get his foot to work again. He has powered through one adversity after another, and today he is a successful elementary teacher in Austin, Texas.

His stubbornness is still in play over a decade later. A few months after the accident, Dave's peripheral nerve surgeon told him that if the nerve that kept him from lifting his foot and toes didn't recover in two years - it probably wasn't going to heal. For the last two years, Dave has forced himself to walk up stairs at home with no foot brace, plus he borrowed a tens unit for his leg to stimulate nerve growth. Even though his right calf has atrophied badly, he is finally able to lift his toes after a decade. Years ago, the surgeon suspected that a fall from his hospital bed broke his tailbone and damaged the nerve near his pelvis. It takes nerves a long time to grow to your feet if you are 6'2".

Dave is married and is a fabulous dad to my three-year-old granddaughter. And, she clearly has a similar stubborn personality – for which I believe he is grateful.

Nancy – one son and one daughter; grandchildren

Cathryn J. Lombardo

A Mother's Wisdom

A Mom's Haiku to My Two Plus Five Words of Wisdom

<u>The Son</u>
So young and clueless,
I see a little bundle, stretch
my arms to take him.

My firstborn, my gift.
An unexpected blessing
safe in my glad heart.

Six years pass, Hot Wheels,
Lincoln Logs, Legos, Cap guns,
fights with neighbor kids.

Don't be too bossy, I advise.
Words of wisdom? Oh, you bet.

Cathryn J. Lombardo

The Daughter
I, older, wiser,
a new bundle to hold. I'd
forgotten how small.

No matter how loud
she cried, my little girl claimed
her place in my heart.

Did I think I'd love
the second less than the first?
Was I that silly?

One day she huffed, our
neighbor wasn't a real man,
not nice to small girls.

My advice? Ignore the jerk.
Words of wisdom? Oh, you bet.

Both
Little League and
gymnastics. Fast bikes, cute clothes.
Years speed by too fast.

Failed goals, broken hearts, lost dreams.
Words of wisdom? Oh, I hope.

A Mother's Wisdom

The Son
High school's done, college
now. The future waits for him.
He has other plans.

Oh my, she's the one.
Soon we have a wedding day.
My son becomes a man.

Triple jobs, fun arcades.
Youth doesn't sacrifice fun.
Tokens don't come cheap.

Got no money, not enough time.
Words of wisdom? Who listens?

The Grandsons
He's here, son's firstborn.
Bright and strong, loved by many.
Generations grow.

Big wheels, then hot wheels.
A new brother joins the crew.
Fights over toys ensue.

Be nice, you'll soon be best friends.
Words of wisdom? Huh? What words?

Cathryn J. Lombardo

The Granddaughter
New job, bigger house.
Do they need a little girl?
Their auntie thinks so.

Red hair, blue eyes and
not left handed. Sweet honey,
the pampered youngest.

Someday you'll like your brothers.
Words of wisdom? Sure, you bet.

The Daughter
In high school now and
wants to shine. She's better than
she thinks she could be.

Adonis arrives,
Ken and Barbie hold hands and
have a grand wedding.

A grand house, too far away.
Word of wisdom? They think not.

The Grandson
Delayed for so long,
her dream of sweet motherhood.
He's finally here.

A Mother's Wisdom

Tiny hands and feet,
snuffling up to Mommy's chest.
Hello there, small champ.

Thomas the Train is his favorite
until years pass and Halo takes over.

The Granddaughter
Who wants a baby sis?
He does, more than he admits.
He has his own room.

She does too but her
bed's a crib and he sleeps in
a real big boy bed.

Love sister, she'll love you back.
Words of wisdom? See that frown.

The Wise Words
Mother's wisdom may
be a myth. Who knows it all?
Very few of us.

Our children grow so
fast they make us wonder who
really learned the most.

Cathryn J. Lombardo

Did wisdom pass over and
back, like alternating current?
Who was truly wise?

Trust our own inner guidance.
Words of wisdom? Oh, you bet.

Connie – one daughter and one son; five grandchildren

A Mother's Wisdom

Life Isn't Fair... Suck It Up!

What isn't fair about life? Well...everything. In fact, when you think about it, there is almost nothing that is what you and I might consider truly "fair." So what? It isn't meant to be. One of my favorite sayings in life is, "Pull up your big girl panties and deal with it." Actually, the same applies for boxers. Just suck it up and deal!

So...how do you do that? Just exactly how are you supposed to "Suck it up"? Let me show you by giving you some examples of things that just aren't fair.

Competition: There's always a winner and a loser, seldom a tie. Even when there is a tie, have you ever noticed how everyone feels cheated somehow? Whatever the outcome, someone's not happy. So get used to both outcomes and learn how to do both well. Is winning better? Well, duh...of course it is. But you can't win them all. Some you win, some you lose, and some get rained out. Some of my greatest epiphanies came from losing, and there may actually be days when you find yourself praying for rain. That's okay. Remember that every challenge generally yields a winner and potentially a loser. But the only time you are a true loser is if you fail to take the high road, be gracious, and try to learn from the experience. Strangely, the way to be a good winner is exactly the same...high road, graciousness, and learning. Do that and you will successfully turn *every* loss into a win; and in those times when you do win the competition, others won't mind quite so much that you won...they might even cheer for you.

Love: Again, sadly, some succeed, some do not. So what? Keep trying. You get back on the horse. Like I said earlier, pull up your big girl panties (or briefs, as case may be) and deal with it. There is no shame in a failed relationship, as long as you have taken the high road. Treat others right, love fairly and with gusto, and if it doesn't work out, take what lessons you can from the relationship and move on. No anger, no revenge, no grudges, and for God's sake, no stalking! It makes you look needy.

Finances: Not everyone can be a Rockefeller. Some will be upper class, some middle class, and some lower class. There is no shame in any financial status, but make sure you are "choosing" to be where you are and not just allowing life or others to determine it for you. Remember, not trying or not making a choice is, by its very nature, a choice to fail.

Employment: There are only so many rocket scientists, pro football players or acting superstars. Not everyone is born to be a Cher, or a Michael Jordan, or a Meryl Streep, or Clint Eastwood. So? Pick something else...pick something you *can* do, something you enjoy. Don't have the beauty or talent for the big screen? Try radio. Can't dribble the ball or run the length of a football field in less than 30 minutes? Try teaching kids who can. Can't carry a tune? Don't know how to make a million dollars? Go into politics, save people from burning buildings, or find someone who can teach you how to make that million. The point is, whatever you do for employment, do it well. Be the best you can be.

Beauty: Okay, so we're not all Miss America material, and we're not all going to end up on the cover of GQ. Again, Suck It Up! It is what it is. But remember—whatever it is, you have the power to make it better. Beauty is easily enhanced by attitude, personality, makeup, a smile, and if all else fails, plastic surgery. But take the easy route first and put on a smile, try a dash of lipstick, and leave laughter wherever you go. You'll be amazed at how gorgeous others will think you are, even though you may not think you see it in the mirror. But please, if you take the plastic surgery route, be conservative. A little goes a long way—if you're doing more than two or three procedures, you've crossed the line into desperation. Get help! Try to focus on what is beautiful about you. Maybe you have a beautiful personality. That will put you miles ahead of everyone else. You'll be amazed at how many doors open to a beautiful personality that will not open to a gorgeous face with nothing behind it. You focus on being the best you that you can be and your beauty will shine through. Would I lie? It's the truth. I promise!

Intelligence: Einstein I'm not. Neither was my mother or my father, nor theirs before them. So chances are good that Einstein isn't in your genes either. Were you cheated? Yep. Oh well. It doesn't matter. You were born with everything you need to be the best *you* possible. Use it. You've got a huge bag of resources at your fingertips. There is education and street smarts and common sense, all of which combined together can make you *smarter* than the average Einstein. There are plenty of extremely intelligent people who can't tie their shoestrings or remember to come in out of the rain. You strive to be balanced and do the best you can each day. Use your street smarts and your common sense and you'll look like the smartest guy on the block. Trust me on this!

Height: This is sort of like ordering Chinese food off a menu. Some want it hot, some want it mild, some want it sweet, and some want it sour. So with height, I can almost guarantee you, whatever you got, it ain't enough of what you want. Big deal. If you're too short, stand up straight. It'll make you look taller and people will perceive you as someone with pride, someone who isn't intimidated by his/her lack of height. If you're too tall, strangely enough, the solution is the same—stand up tall. People won't perceive you as shorter than you really are, but they will be awed by what they see, which is a person that is proud of what he/she was given in life. These rules apply equally for both men and women. Be proud of whatever it is you got because you got it for a reason. Show the world you know how to use it.

Age: Now, this is a strange one because we all start out equal on this. But as we age, we begin to see an imbalance. Others are older and act like they are wiser when we are young. Deal with it...they are. As we age, we begin to envy or resent those that are younger because their skin doesn't sag or they have so many years ahead. We resent that our eyes are failing or our hearing is deteriorating or we can't remember what the hell we came into that room for. So what? You'll still be wiser than those youngsters, you'll still have all those experiences to draw on (or remember fondly). No matter what your age, you will find there are benefits that far outweigh the negatives, no matter what end of the scale you are on. So while it might seem unfair at times, we all start out equal and we all end up ahead in one way or another.

Okay, I guess that's about all I have to say on the subject; and if that's all I ever leave to my son, my nieces, and my grandchildren, then it's not a bad legacy. You learn these lessons and I believe you will have everything you need in life—everything you need to be the smartest, richest, most beautiful, most athletic, most successful, most intelligent, most loving you that you can be. After all is said and done, no one could ever ask any more of you than that. In fact, to achieve that much is probably the pinnacle of a successful life. It will put you ahead of ninety percent of the people on this planet.

You see, I believe it is all part of God's master plan. None of us are put on this earth to be the best athlete ever, or the prettiest beauty contestant ever, or the richest person ever—that's why records that are set are almost always eventually broken. I believe we were put here to simply be the best that each of us can be. The good news is each and every one of us was given *all* the tools we need to be exactly that. So strive to be the best at everything you do and be thrilled to be the best *you* ever.

Not fair? Of course not—and thank God it isn't!

Suck it up and just be the best *you* ever created.

All my love,
Yaya

Kayce - one son; four grandsons

A Mother's Wisdom - Iris

Since the beginning of my married life, I have moved eight times. The reason I'm writing about my moves is because they have affected my becoming who I am today. I learned early on to make the most of each situation. I did this by meeting and making friends, discovering new places, learning about my surroundings, exploring new interests – always looking on the "BRIGHT" side – thinking positive.

Learning from my mother, I was slow to make any judgments of those whom I met. Therefore, it was easy to make and keep friends. Sometimes it was a challenge, but challenges can broaden us from the inside out.

At this time in my life, I still say, "Let's have an adventure" – like going tent camping at age *eighty*!!

Losing my two husbands (both named Roger!) has been very sad indeed. Going through the loss and pain, not once but twice, started me on my "Faith Journey." Because of my grief process, these two Bible verses have been very meaningful to me:

> Romans, 8:26: *"Likewise the Spirit helps us in our weakness; for we do not know how to pray as we ought, but the Spirit himself intercedes for us with sighs too deep for words."*[11]

> Romans, 8: 28: *"We know that in everything God works for good with those who love him, who are called according to his purpose."*[11] (This verse helped me through the loss of my first Roger.)

This was meaningful when my second Roger was asked to leave his job at Ketchikan General Hospital:

> Psalm, 46:1: *"God is our refuge and strength, a very present help in trouble."*[11]

> Psalm, 46:10: *"Be still, and know that I am God. I am exalted among the nations, I am exalted in the earth!"*[11]

When I moved to Jacksonville, OR in 1999 where I would live close to my oldest sister and her husband, the Bible verse from Jeremiah, 29:11: *"For I know the plans I have for you, says the Lord, plans for welfare and not for evil, to give you a future and a hope."*[11] was my theme verse because God had indeed had this move in His plan. I continue to live in Jacksonville where my many friends and family keep me busy and well-loved!

Here are other wisdoms I would like to share:

Be Real.
Say it like it is!
Smile and you will receive smiles.
Positive thinking, in most cases of life situations, has been helpful.
Do not worry – take each day/situation and live in the NOW.
Treat yourself with flowers.
Be yourself – not phony.
Be a good listener.

Iris – one daughter and one son; five grandchildren; four great-grandchildren

Cathryn J. Lombardo

A Most Wise Woman - My Mother

Darlene is her name, and, boy, did she earn her stripes. With four kids and a husband who acted like a kid himself upon occasion, she really had her hands full. At times she was a stay-at-home mother; but more often as the oldest, I remember being a latch-key kid after school. She not only went back to school to earn her degree, but went on to work to help support the family. Or was it to get away from us heathens? Somehow I think a little of both.

As we grew up, we had our "times." With three girls and one boy, huge dramas were going on at any given moment, not to mention the chaos, but my mom handled it all with her indomitable spirit and grace.

Okay, now it was my turn at parenthood. My son had just turned fourteen and I was being paid back in a huge way for the drama I had brought to the table when I was that age. He had fallen in with a pretty rough group of kids and was acting out in a big way. No matter how hard we tried to bring him back, he was determined to learn and live his life the hard way. His step-father and I were frightened for him. So, after many tears and conversations, we decided to send him to his biological father who lived in my home town in Oregon. We prayed the small town atmosphere and the support of my family: cousins, grandmother, grandfather and aunts and uncles would help in my son's life decisions.

Of course, he wasn't happy at all being separated from his fellow hooligans, and put up a huge fight which tore me apart. It was the hardest day of my life when we sent him away. On one particularly hard day afterward, I was crying to my mother, telling her how scared I was that I was going to lose him forever. What she said to me, I have repeated to young women throughout my life who were going through the same thing. It was this bit of wisdom that got me through all of the drama and hurt:

> *"He will always come back to you because of the good foundation you laid down for him while you were raising him. You gave him a great life with all the right basics. He will come back. He knows right from wrong."*

A Mother's Wisdom

She was absolutely correct. My son has turned into the best son a mother could have as well as an incredible husband and father. I was truly blessed to have such a wise mother to impart such wisdom during a traumatic period of my life.

Thanks, Mom.

Jaylene – one son; one grandson

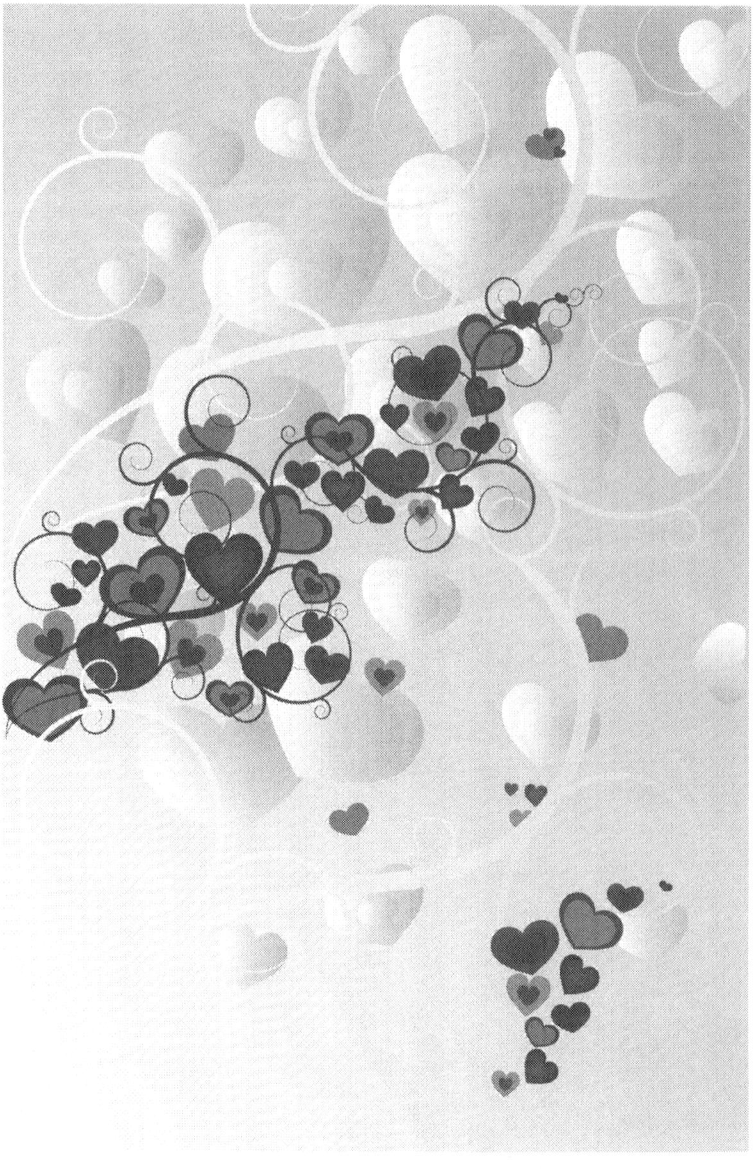

A Mother's Wisdom

To My Children and Grandchildren

I sat down one day babysitting the newest grandbaby and the following thoughts flowed:

Remember that nothing stays the same. There is nothing more constant than change. Thus, when you are dismayed and upset with your situation, remember it is not forever. Keep the hope. At the same time, those delightful and wondrous moments of your life do not last either. So enjoy them whenever and wherever they pop up. Again, always hold hope in your heart.

Secondly, kindness goes a long way in this life; kindness, along with politeness. Have the phrases "thank-you" and "please" and "May I?" and "I'm sorry" handy on the tip of your tongue.

Treat everyone the same; from the busboy at a restaurant to the owner of the restaurant; from the woman who waits on you at the gas station to the Queen of England. Your father/grandfather does this really well, follow his example.

Help those less fortunate than yourself – be generous toward all when it comes to kindness, moral support, love.

> **NOTE**: Remember that you are always loved, that you are a unique child of the universe.

Next, seek to do good always. This thought is expounded upon by Mark Twain with this quote: *"Always do right. This will gratify some people and astonish the rest."*[12] I heard this quote at my college graduation, some thirty-four years ago, and have never forgotten it. May you astonish the world!!!

Also, when you do something good, don't brag about it... do good deeds when nobody is looking; where nobody knows you do them – do them for the satisfying feelings it arouses in you. You can share your good deeds with God!!!

> **NOTE**: Cultivate your friendships. Cherish those friends who listen to you yet don't try to tell you what to do.

When it comes to your "physical self," exercise your whole life through, AND eat as many veggies and fruits as you can. One of you once wrote me a tiny, two-page book which read: Page 1 – "Eat Less" and Page 2 – "Exercise More." This tiny book says it all when it comes to weight control.

Your great-grandmother and great-great grandmother (my grandmother) always said, "Moderation in all things." And she lived this credo, too. Her name was Lila. She lived to be ninety-three years old. This is wisdom from an elder worth listening to.

Enjoy the seasons of the year; the heat of summer, the brilliance of fall, the gray of winter, and the gorgeous green shades of spring. The seasons mark your years and renew your spirit.

Enjoy the holidays and birthdays – keep your expectations low for the holidays, and simply take in and ponder in your heart the blessings that are there.

Furthermore, save your sweetest and gentlest self for your spouse, if you do marry, and for all of those who are closest to you. Be sweet and gentle to your children, if you have them. Sometimes this is hard to do, but it pays off each day and creates a nourishing home life.

Help take care of the earth. It's important for future generations–like your children's generation, your grandchildren's generation, and all the generations to come.

NOTE: Take delight in the living of each day – enjoy the sunrises and sunsets, the starry skies at night, and everyone from soft, cooing newborn babies to eccentric old people!!!

Somewhere along the way I heard this: *"Patience is a virtue to be desired."*[13] Seek to be patient, beginning with yourself. Be patient with yourself and what you hope to be and achieve in this life. Talk to yourself kindly and with love. Emphasize the positive. Laugh a lot (your father/grandfather and I do this every day). And see the sunny side of life, as the old song goes, *"Keep on the sunny side of life."*[14]

As far as spouses go – pick someone who is able and willing to share what I call the "butt work" of life: taking out the garbage, washing the dishes, cleaning the toilets, vacuuming, grocery shopping, balancing the checkbook, making the decisions of a household – sharing the load in this area makes life much less of a "job" and more like a shared journey.

Trust your feelings and allow yourself to feel. Honor your feelings. You are entitled to them. Feelings are not good or bad in and of themselves. What you do with your feelings and the actions you take in response to your feelings - now that's where "the rubber hits the road." That's where you make the right and wrong decisions, and all the decisions that are shades of gray, neither right or wrong, but better or worse.

Also, trust your instincts but be willing to listen to the wisdom and knowledge of others, and the wisdom and knowledge of your elders.

My favorite phrase from the Bible is found in the book of John, 8:32: *"... and you will know the truth, and the truth will make you free."*[15] Be a seeker of truth!!!

> **NOTE**: Remember that love is more a verb and not a noun. Love is something you do more than something you say.

Finally, and I had to look this up, I quote from Judith Martin's book, *Miss Manners*.[16] In her book, Ms. Martin has folks writing questions to her and then she answers them.

> One person wrote this:
> *"Dear Miss Manners: Do you have any guidelines that will help me to feel correct in all situations?"*
>
> And her reply was this:
> *"Gentle Reader:*
> *Yes, two, both of which were given to her by her Uncle Henry when Miss Manners was a mere slip of a girl. They have served her well in all the vicissitudes of life ever since. They are:*
> *1. Don't.*
> *2. Be sure not to forget to."*

My dear children and grandchildren, there it is in a nutshell - "Don't" & "Be sure not to forget to":

> ***Don't*** steal, lie, slander, murder, be mean, gossip, be petty, be cranky, whine, etc.

> ***Be sure not to forget to*** say "thank you," to write thank you notes, to say "I love you" a lot, and to hug, nurture, listen, work hard, study hard, dance, laugh, etc.

I love you so much!

Love, Mom/Grandma

P.S. Use a dictionary all the time. It keeps life interesting. Go look up *vicissitude*!!!

Nancy – one son and one daughter; six grandchildren

A Mother's Wisdom - Bette

What I learned from my children, and augmented by my grandchildren, is the true meaning of unconditional love. To me there's nothing like a baby. Our first baby was stillborn and my feeling for her and my three adult children continues to swell my heart the older I become.

Years ago, when my children were young, my hour of quiet time came at the end of the evening between eleven p.m. and midnight. I'd have a Pepsi and a cigarette (I didn't quit smoking until my first grandson was born and I decided I wanted to live to see him grow up—he's nineteen now and in college). I'd watch the news for half an hour and then I'd watch the opening segment of Johnny Carson. I don't think I missed one night during the twenty-five years he was on TV. There were many times when he'd interview someone famous who had been married numerous times, led a selfish, miserable life, did drugs and even had children who were messed up and perhaps had a child who died of an overdose. Johnny would ask, "Any regrets?" And the person often replied, "No!" I'd freak out—how does anyone go through life without regrets? It's part of life.

I regret I had to cook, clean, do dishes and laundry, work in the yard and do all the things a housewife has to do to run an efficient home. Unfortunately, I was raised to give June Cleaver some competition. I wish my mother hadn't given me such a strong sense of responsibility. I wish I had taken the children to the movies more often, saved enough money to take vacations, taken the kids to Branson for Thanksgiving, Disneyland for Easter, and Europe for the summer. Not that we didn't do some fun things, like take a motor home from Concord and Lexington to Boston, Plymouth, Newport and Groton. We went to beaches, amusement parks, and boating with the grandparents, but mostly we visited relatives on our vacation. We sent all three children to Europe on class trips during spring break, but I wish we could have afforded to take them ourselves. Of course, I'm sure they had a better time without us, but I regret missing that experience with them.

I regret ever yelling or disciplining them when I was angry, and sorry I didn't stay upstairs and read three stories to them at bedtime instead of one or two because I had to do the dishes and pack lunches for the next day.

And I regret never having finished filling out their baby books or taking more photographs and home movies of them. For the grandchildren, whom I love to spoil and keep in touch with by phone, email, and visits, I kept a special file on my Zip drive for each of them. I kept a record, from the day they were born until their tenth birthday, of all the funny things they said and did, and places where we went and things we did together. This year I gave the youngest her booklet. When I'm gone, they will have their book of memories and lots of photograph albums to keep.

We emphasized education for the children and grandchildren so they can afford to do all the things they'd like to do. And, of my children and grandchildren, I can honestly say they never have, nor could they ever do, anything to disappoint me. My love is unconditional, thanks to them.

Another regret that I have is that not all problems in life have happy endings, like in my romance novels. And, as I enter into my twilight years, I regret that I will have to leave my family. Not because I'm afraid to die, but because no one will ever love my children like I do. I want to be around in case they need me. I believe in the hereafter and hope that somehow they will know I'm up there looking after them...always.

Two things I can think of that I always emphasized to my children: one was when they were old enough to drive, and even to this day, on their way out I say, "Don't drink, and never drink and drive." A little guilt never hurt....

The second thing I always tell my children when things go bad, or hearts are broken, or jobs are lost and they don't have enough money, is that someone else is worse off than they are and bad things happen to good people. I ask them to make a decision about what can be done to make things better and remind them, "It's not the end of the world. I'll let you know when that is going to happen."

Bette – two sons and one daughter; five grandchildren

A Mother's Wisdom

For My Children: An Alphabet of Lessons I've Learned from Life

My Dear Children,
My mother, our beloved Umma, gave me lots of advice when I was growing up. In fact, she had advice for every occasion. Here are just a few of her gems:

"Always wear clean underwear in case you're in a car accident." Now, I have to be honest with you. If I were in an accident, the last thing I'd think about would be pristine panties.

"Don't pick your nose." This one is actually great advice, and I taught you the same thing. Thank you for listening!

"Don't sass." My friend Pammy Sue was allowed to talk back all she wanted. I tried it once, and immediately found out that the right hand of God is really my mother.

"Stand up straight." When you're 5'10" tall and all your friends are 5'4" or shorter, it's slouch or walk on your knees. At least this was the excuse I gave Mom. She didn't buy it.

"Don't whine." As far as Umma was concerned, whining was the worst possible sound a person could make.

"Always carry a dime." Yes, this actually paid for an emergency phone call.

"If you fall off your bike come right home so I can put some iodine on you." The iodine scared me more than falling.

"Clean your plate." Probably not as good an idea now as it was then.

"Don't fight with your sister." I'm sure we'll outgrow it.

"Don't you dare say you're bored." And if we did, there were lots of chores to alleviate our boredom.

Umma and Papa managed to raise me without too much trauma, and I hope you didn't suffer too much with me as your mother. Both of you are incredible, caring, intelligent adults. I love you and am so proud of you! You already know what my advice will be. You grew up with it.

****

As a librarian, I have a tendency to organize information. So here's an alphabet of lessons I've learned from life and tried to pass on to you. Please let me know if I accidentally skipped one of these when you were little!

Accept people for what they are.
Don't try to change people. It's like the old saying, "Don't teach a pig how to sing. It is a waste of your time, and it annoys the pig."

Be thankful for what you have.
I once heard a Holocaust survivor say, "Be thankful for the dirty dishes in your sink. It means you have someplace to live and you've had something to eat."

Celebrate successes and learn from failures.
Turn your failures into successes by learning from them. I know, that sounds like something you'd hear from a feel-good guru. But it's true. One success after another gives you no coping skills for when that inevitable failure happens.

Dwell in the present.
Enjoy the now. The past is over. The future isn't here yet. As someone pointed out, the present is just that, a gift.

Embrace diversity.
The world has an exciting mixture of races, cultures, and religions. Learn from them. All of us have as many similarities as we do differences. Maybe more. We are all God's children.

Forgive easily.
Grudges and hatred will make you spiritually and physically ill. They suck up your energy and make you lose your focus.

Give God the glory.
He gave us everything.

Help the helpless.
The poor, the elderly, the physically disabled, the mentally ill—don't let them become invisible to you.

Ignore the naysayers.
Be the Little Engine that Could. Don't listen to people who tell you something is impossible.

Joke and jest and see the joy in life.
A good sense of humor will get you through just about anything.

Know yourself.
Polonius isn't the most likable Shakespearean character, but his advice to his son, Laertes, is sound:
> *"This above all: to thine own self be true,*
> *And it must follow, as the night the day,*
> *Thou canst not then be false to any man."*[17]

Make family a higher priority than work.
The regret that I will carry to my grave is that I spent so much time at work. Don't make the same mistake.

Never go to bed angry.
Anger is another soul-sucker. Make peace with the person you're mad at—even if it's yourself—before you turn in for the night.

Obey the Golden Rule.
Even better, observe the Platinum Rule: "Treat others the way they want to be treated."

Practice random acts of kindness every day.
In the 1700's, John Wesley said, "Do all the good you can, by all the means you can, in all the ways you can, in all the places you can, at all the times you can, to all the people you can, as long as ever you can."[18] Three hundred years later, it's still a good idea.

Quell all thoughts of self-doubt.
Remember—you are special. God doesn't make trash. Speaking of which...

Recycle.
Our Earth is a finite resource.

Stay close to family, especially each other.
Siblings have a special bond. Don't ever break it.

Tell family and friends you love them, and tell them often.
That way, they don't have to wonder.

Use the talent God gave you.
There's a reason you have it.

Value your true friends.
A real friend is one of the best gifts you'll ever get.

Work hard, but take time to play.
Keep your life in balance. Your mind and body will thank you.

X-out negativity.
Stay away from negative people and thoughts. They create breeding grounds for self-doubt and dissatisfaction.

A Mother's Wisdom

Yell for your favorite team, but never at other people.
Once they're out of your mouth, words can never be taken back. It's even worse when you've yelled them in anger.

Zero in on what's important in your life.
As you get older, you'll realize how little time we have. Use it wisely.

So there you have it. That's my best advice for you. Oh, and by the way, if you fall off your bike, come right home. I'm always here for you. Without iodine.

Love you forever,
Mom

Shelley – one son, one daughter

Cathryn J. Lombardo

A Mother's Wisdom

Here's to the Journey!!
On BEING your Mom

The love and journey we share as mother and daughters is sacred. It is a love interwoven with memories shared, love in the present moments and dreams of the future.
We are connected by an invisible strand of energy that is made of this LOVE.
It is FOREVER!

The greatest honor I've had in my life is to be your Mom.
You've taught me so many things—especially how LOVE manifests spiritually and emotionally.

Believe in the beauty and potential of ALL!!
Hold fast to your inner wisdom and TRUST your intuition.
BELIEVE and know how sacred LOVE and LIFE are.

Cathryn J. Lombardo

Love never dies. Pay It Forward every chance you get. Look at intentions and make choices using your heart along with discernment.

Remember—you're TRUE BLUES!!!!

You are never alone because I'll always be here for you. Being your Mom has been the most sacred calling I've ever had!! Know that your Dad loves and cherishes you both more than ANYTHING in this world!! You'll ALWAYS be his little girls!!!

Your thoughts are my thoughts and your dreams are my dreams.

We will ALWAYS be connected and we are ALL connected. Remember that wherever there are people there are always opportunities for moments of kindness.

As you continue down this road of life, choose your paths carefully. Allow JOY, LOVE & LAUGHTER IN!!!!

Choose FORGIVENESS and COMPASSION every chance you can. Only say you are sorry IF you mean it.

Find a 'TA DA" moment each and every day.
(And especially on ordinary days—it makes them EXTRA ORDINARY!!!!)

A Mother's Wisdom

Celebrate waking up with the sunrise
and give thanks and gratitude when the sun is setting.
We are
All connected.

I love Maya Angelo's quote: *"I've learned that people will forget what you said, people will forget what you did, but people will never forget how you made them feel."*[19]

Remember that LOVE is a verb!!

Don't EVER apologize for FEELING!!

I believe we're all spiritual beings having a physical experience.

We choose to be together and I know we always will.

Here's to flutterbyes, our 4-legged friends; bootcamp, beaches, & turtles!! Blues & Golds, Greens & Oranges; Softball, Lake Powell & Rocky Point; picture-taking; concerts under the stars and most of all
connecting at the heart.

Keep this mantra about women in your soul from Kris Radish's book: *Hearts on a String*,[20] where a little girl and her Nana are talking about something very precious and sacred between women.

"The woman tells the attentive girl about the precious, beautiful sweet string that connects all women. She tells her great-granddaughter that the string is so pure and light that many women cannot see it. The string is a powerful force, my sweet girl. It allows women to lean into one another and find a sister when they need one. The string can never be broken. You can use it to pull yourself up, to pull yourself forward, or to steady the place where you must remain. Are you sure all women see this string, Nana? The little girl asks. Oh yes! Her great-grandmother exclaims. If they dare to see and feel, if they build a world for their hearts and lives that comes from the designs of their own souls.
They can see it."
You are my heart strings,
dear daughters...

Memories are incredible and
making more are what allows our
Spirits to smile!!!

Believe in Angels!!
Believe in the magic of "SPIRIT."

Remember: the circle of LIFE is endless. Thank you for loving and respecting your grandparents and allowing them to be such an integral part of your lives.

A Mother's Wisdom

Blessings to you both as you begin your own life's journeys with the men that you've chosen.

Create good habits—they're as hard to break as the bad ones.

Listen with your heart and don't let anyone destroy your passion for LIFE!!!

Enjoy the journey!!

Smile at ALL pregnant woman!!

No act of kindness, no matter how small, is every wasted.

I also love this quote from Maya Angelo:
"A woman in harmony with her Spirit is like a river flowing. She goes where she will without pretense and arrives at her destination, prepared to be HERSELF and ONLY HERSELF."[19]

And my last reflections I want to share once again with you:
The reading with which we open all our
"Catch the Spirit" seminars:

As you journey through life,
Choose your destinations well,
But do not hurry there.
You will arrive soon enough.

Cathryn J. Lombardo

Wander the back roads and
forgotten paths,
Keeping your destination in your heart
Like the fixed point of a compass.
Seek out new voices, strange sights,
And ideas foreign to your own.
Such things are riches for the soul.
And if, upon arrival,
You find that your destination
Is not exactly as you had dreamed,
Do not be disappointed.
Think of all you would have missed
But for the journey there,
And know that the true worth
Of the travels lies not in where
You come to be at journey's end,
But in whom you come to be
Along the way.[21]
      Written by Jorge Heredia

Mary – two daughters

Acknowledgments

This book could not have been made without the assistance of Ruth Perkins, artist extraordinaire. She and I have worked together on many projects of which her artwork and creativity have been astounding pieces to the completion of the whole. Thank you, Ruth! You know how dear to my heart you are.

My undying gratitude to Kristin Tualla – truly a gift from the gods! - for her advice in the preparation of this book. She so selflessly gave of her time and acumen to one who knew just enough to hang herself! I am in your debt, my dear.

To my husband, Tom, who has stood by me and my writing career for longer than he cares to admit. We are finally on the road, darlin'! My love to you always ....

Contributing Author Websites

Page 1 – *Advice to My Child*, Laurie Schnebly-Campbell;
website: www.BookLaurie.com

Page 15 – *The Magical World of Motherhood*, Shannon Zweig (w/a: Jami Gray);
blogs: jamigray.wordpress.com and 7evildwarves.wordpress.com

Page 25 – *For My Sons*, Cathryn J. Lombardo;
website: www.cathrynjlombardo.com

Page 43 – *Motherhood is Survival of the Craziest*, Stacey Goitia;
website: anastasiafoxe.com

Page 57 – *For Ian*, Donna Marie Del Grosso; on Facebook

Page 63 – *My Family's Particular Wisdom*, Jeanne Cook;
websites: www.ginikoch.com, and Raphael's Village www.raphaelsvillage.com
blog: thegreatcorrupter.blogspot.com.

Page 81 – *A Mother's Wisdom*, Dr. Valeria Breiten;
website: www.drvaleria.net

Page 85 – *Children Are Hilarious*, Kris Tualla;
website: www.KrisTualla.com;
blog: kristualla.wordpress.com

Page 95 – *Stubbornness as a Virtue*, Nancy Chaney; (website pending)

Page 101 – *A Mom's Haiku.....*, Connie Flynn;
website: ConnieFlynn.com;
blog: bootcamp-classroom.blogspot.com

Page 107 – *Life Isn't Fair...Suck It Up!*, Kayce Lassiter;
website: www.kaycelassiter.com;
blog: www.butterscotchmartinigirls.com

Page 127 – *A Mother's Wisdom-Bette*, Elizabeth McNicholas;
website: www.linkedin.com

Page 131 – *For My Children....*, Shelley Mosley;
website: www.deborahshelley@mindspring.com

Page 139 – *Here's to the Journey!!....*, Mary J. Neuman;
neuman@cox.net

Cover Art: Ruth Perkins, also writing as Lily Rose Moon
website: http://LilyRoseMoon.com;
artist's blog: http://LilyRoseMoonArt.blogspot.com

Back Cover Photo: SC Lawrence Photography.
website: www.sclawrence.com

References

Nurturing Others and Yourself
  1. New World Dictionary by Webster.
  2. "Six Degrees of Separation"-- Movie-was released in 1993.
  3. "Friendship Quotes" www.friendship.com.au/quotes/

For My Sons
  4. Saying found on greeting card from Cannon Beach, Oregon.
  5. John Lennon (1940 - 1980), Lyrics from song: *"Beautiful Boy,"* album: Double Fantasy (1980).
  6. Sir Walter Scott (1771 - 1832), *Marmion, Canto vi. Stanza 17.*

From the Journal of Gypsy La Fai
  7. Victor Hugo, Histoire d'un Crime (History of a Crime) (written 1852, published 1877).
  8. Lao, tzu (604BC-531BC), *The Way of Lao tzu.*

For Ian
  9. *Yes (band) The Yes Album, "I've Seen All Good People"* as found on sheet music: *"Your Move,"* c1971, 1983 TOPOGRAPHIC MUSIC LIMITED All rights for the World administered by WB MUSIC CORP.

My Dearest Babies
  10. Franklin, Benjamin. Actual quote: "A spoonful of honey will catch more flies than a gallon of vinegar" (1744). Read more: http://quotationsbook.com/quote/38111/#ixzz1JXS56e6m

A Mother's Wisdom

A Mother's Wisdom-Iris
   11. *Bible-* Revised Standard Version, Thomas Nelson & Sons, 1952.

To My Children and Grandchildren
   12. Twain, Mark. US Humorist, novelist, short story author, & wit. (1835-1910) in a speech given at Greenpoint Presbyterian Church, Brooklyn, N.Y., 1901.
   13. Bierce, Ambrose. Actual quote: "Patience is a minor form of despair, disguised as a virtue." Ambrose Bierce Quotes, WorldofQuotes.com.
   14. Blenkhorn, Ada. Song writer, *"On the Sunny Side of Life,"* in 1899; music by J. Howard Entwisle.
   15. The *New Revised Standard Version of the Bible*; Edited by Bruce M. Metzger & Roland E. Murphy; Oxford University Press, New York, NY; 1991.
   16. Martin, Judith. *Miss Manners' Guide to Excruciatingly Correct Behavior*; illustrated by Gloria Kamen; Warner Books, New York, NY; 1982.

For My Children – An Alphabet of Lessons.....
   17. Shakespeare, William. *The Tragedy of Hamlet, Prince of Denmark*. Act I, Scene 3, Lines 78-80. Massachusetts Institute of Technology. Web. 2 Feb, 2003. http://shakespeare.mit.edu/hamlet/full.html.
   18. Wesley, John. *A Collection of Hymns for the Use of the People called Methodists*. London: unk, 1780.

Here's to the Journey!!
   19. Maya Angelo quotes; one found on a card and the other on a poster.
   20. Radish, Kris. *Hearts on a String*; Bantam Books, an imprint of The Random House Publishing Group, a division of Random House, Inc., New York. Copyright, 2010.
   21. Heredia, Jorge. *"As you journey through life...."* as told by Toby Frost/Columnist, GateHouse News Service, Posted Sep 30, 2009 @ 12:54 PM on website:
   http://www.wickedlocal.com/lincoln/news/lifestyle/columnists/

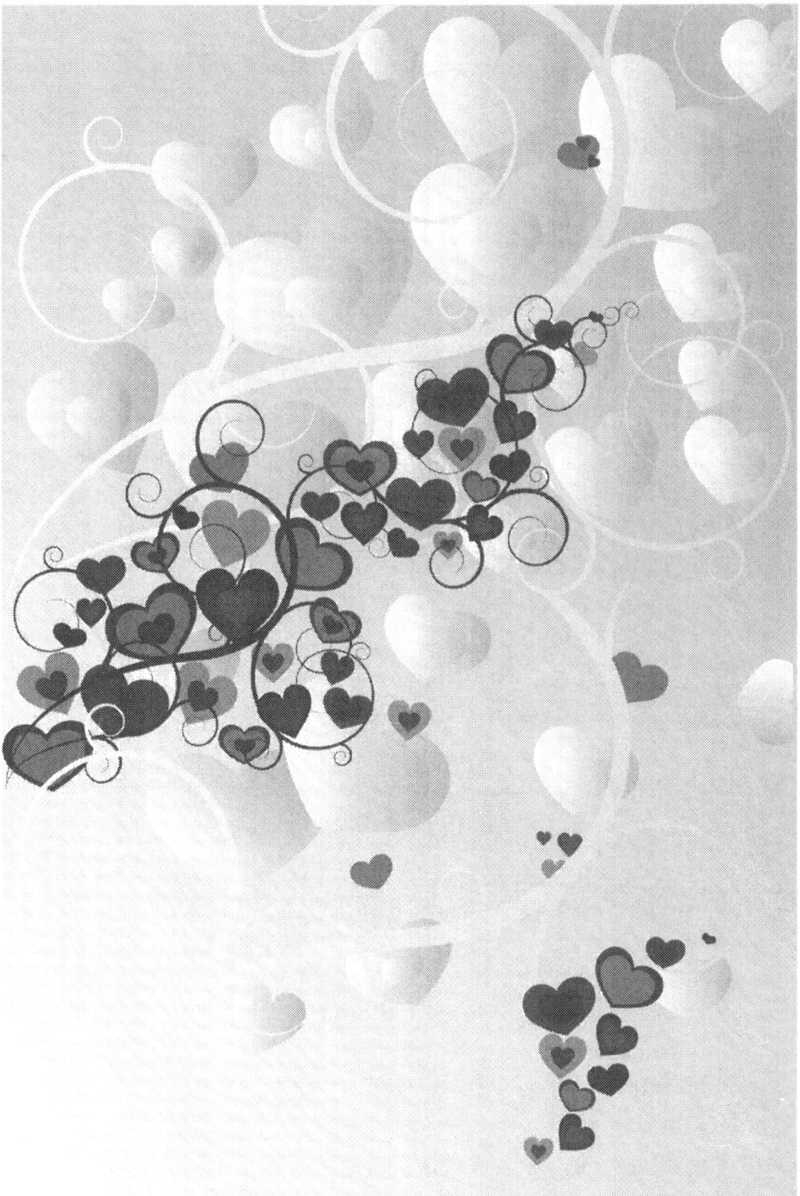

Notes:

Made in the USA
Lexington, KY
11 December 2016